PSYCHEDELIC COLLECTIBLES

of the 1960s & 1970s

PSYCHEDELIC COLLECTIBLES
of the 1960s & 1970s

AN ILLUSTRATED PRICE GUIDE

SUSANNE WHITE

PHOTOGRAPHS BY
David B. Rye

Wallace-Homestead Book Company
Radnor, Pennsylvania

Designed by Anthony Jacobson
Manufactured in the United States of America

Library of Congress Cataloging in Publication Data
White, Susanne, 1959–
    Psychedelic collectibles of the 1960s and 1979s / Susanne White;
photographs by David B. Rye.
        p.   cm.
    ISBN 0-87069-541-X
    1. Psychedelic art—United States—Collectors and collecting.
2. Art, Modern—20th century—United States—Collectors and
collecting.   3. Hallucinogenic drugs—Influence.   I. Title.
N6512.5.P79W47   1990
709'.73'075—dc20   89-51555
                                                        CIP

1 2 3 4 5 6 7 8 9 0   9 8 7 6 5 4 3 2 1 0

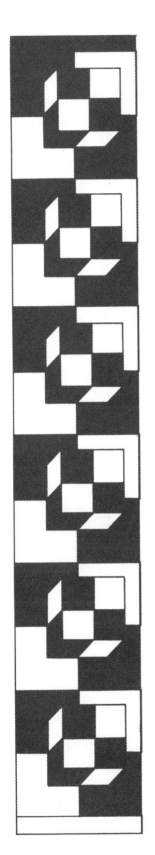

Contents

Preface

 Hello. I'm going to be your guide on this magical mystery tour through the wonderful world of psychedelic stuff.

There once was a time of exuberance in color, pattern, and sound. A time of love, peace, war, and social revolution. Of flowers and guns. Some people look back at that time and are glad it's over. Some have fond memories. Some can't remember a darn thing due to their personal exuberance at the time. Kids who weren't born yet wonder what it was like. I was born in 1959, and I sat in front of the TV and watched it all go by without getting personally involved. We got *Lite* magazine and I read it. I hated to see those pictures from Vietnam. I didn't understand the art much, since I was more involved in the primitive realism style of grade school. But I liked the colors.

I still like the colors.

Acknowledgments

 I'd like to thank a bunch of great people who've helped so much with information, and allowed us to photograph their things. In alphabetical order:

Tom Anderson from New Jersey, with a collection of Tiny Tim, political, fast food, toys, rock music, and everything; Roberta Batt, M.D. of "Pekl" from Maine. Love the Campbell's Soup dress; Gary Borkan, a dealer from Massachusetts; John Bruno of "Flamingo," Long Island, NY; Our friends "Damama" from California; M. Giovanna Del Buono of "Neat Stuff Ent.," Philadelphia, Pennsylvania, a fun shop—it *is* neat stuff; Mark and Deb of "It's Only Rock 'N' Roll," New York City; Dave Jimenez of "Flashback," Carrboro, North Carolina—a poster connoisseur, dealer, and collector who also does nice tiedyes; Patricia Palumbo of "Mix" from Bridgehampton, New York; Richard Pollard from New York City, who's collection of Peter Max is *almost* as great as mine; Jonathan Pozner from Massachusetts with a collection of fashions; Sandy and Sareva Racher from Maryland who told me about "Granny Takes a Trip"—wish I could have been there; Phillip Roy of Massachusetts, who has the *biggest* collection of smilies I've ever seen; Gary Sohmers of "Wex Rex," Hudson, Massachusetts, who says that he has "wicked excellent records and collectibles"; and Laura Townsend from Ohio.

I'd also like to thank my photographer/husband, David Rye for his help, and for tolerating my "I-wanna-quit" phases of this project.

And thanks to Harry Rinker and Alan Turner of the Chilton Book Company for thinking that this book was a good idea.

PSYCHEDELIC COLLECTIBLES
of the 1960s & 1970s

Introduction: A Quick Art History Lesson

Psychedelic art did not just magically appear in 1965 out of an LSD experiment. Psychedelic art happened just like any other artistic movement. It was a product of its time, and evolved from all previous art.

The psychedelic artists often sought inspiration from all the graphic and formal art that had come before them. Art Nouveau, old advertising graphics, American Indian designs—anything that turned them on would be used for new ideas. Most psychedelic art seems to be directly related to all types of late nineteenth century graphics, from Toulouse-Lautrec to side show posters of the American West.

Toulouse Lautrec and Alphonse Mucha were major influences to the psychedelic art of the 1960s, although they were certainly not the only influences.

Paisleys were a late nineteenth cen-

1

tury/early twentieth century fashion rage in Europe and America and a long standing tradition in India. Swirled colored ink was used for marbelizing the end pages in books from around 1800.

Experiments in color reversal (opposite colors placed right next to each other: red/green; blue/orange; purple/yellow) were done in the 1930s and '40s by Josef Albers. Not surprisingly, poster artist Victor Moscoso had studied with Josef Albers at Yale. And Maxfield Parrish was famous for using a lot of opposite, vibrating color in the early 1900s. Various artists and many primitive cultures around the world have taken advantage of bright, vibrating complementary colors for centuries.

Op art was not new either. Similar patterns can be found on mid-nineteenth century woven coverlets; quilts; American Indian and other tribal cultures' baskets, weavings and beadwork; Oriental rugs, patterns of tiles; inlaid wood designs; and probably more.

Though the nineteenth century doesn't seem to us to be a particularly liberated or wild time, it may have originated the first psychedelic light show. Loie Fuller was a very popular dance star from 1889 to 1927. She performed wearing volumes of diaphanous material, which she moved and swirled around herself *while colored lights were projected on her!*

The "Art Nouveau," "Belle Epoch," "Gay Nineties" final 20 years of the nineteenth century were very much like the psychedelic period of this century. It was the beginning of Modern Art as we know it. Impressionism revolutionized the art world. Photography and electricity made possible some new means of artistic expression. In the 1960s, new inventions in plastics helped make some of the more unusual designs in furniture and clothing

Fig. I–1. Section of a mid-nineteenth century American coverlet; blue/red/white.

possible. In the nineteenth century, people were fascinated by the exploration of the Earth's poles and other strange lands. In the 1960s, people were fascinated by the explorations in space. Both periods were fast moving times, which may have something to do with the unrestrained type of art that was created.

Prices

 This is a price *guide*. It is intended to give people an idea of what things are worth, but these values are only estimates. There are many variables that affect the actual price for which an item will sell. Good quality and design *usually* mean a higher price, but not always. An item may be "wonderful," but if it's common the value will be lower. If an item is rare the price will be higher. In the case of some of the rare Fillmore and Avalon Ballroom posters, graphics may not have much to do with the price.

What's hot and what's not. If the antique and collectible newspapers proclaim, "New auction record price!," there will usually be drastic increases in prices of similar items.

Where things are sold has a lot to do with the price. A major auction gallery in New York should be able to bring a higher price for anything than a farmer's auction in Pennsylvania, and certainly for psychedelic collectibles!

Location also affects price, since some things are easier to find in the places where they originated. Peter Max items are generally cheaper in New York, and more expensive in California, while San Francisco music posters are cheaper in California, and more expensive on the East Coast.

Who is buying also determines price. Dealers have to pay less for merchandise to make a profit when they sell it. Collectors will sometimes pay more, but often they are looking for a bargain, too. Corporate buyers may not care how much they spend, as long as it's the *right thing*.

Finally, it's hard to judge value, when certain things just aren't out there for sale. In a few cases, I have noted this, rather than hazard a guess. Protest posters are definitely rare, but what are they worth?

Keeping Your Collection in Good Shape

Time and a variety of nasty chemicals, insects, fungi, rodents, air, and moisture are all out to destroy your beautiful collection. Your job is to keep your goodies away from them.

PAPER

Paper is the most vulnerable collectible. Newspapers will self-destruct due to the acids in the paper and exposure to air. It will turn yellow and brittle, then just fall apart when you try to touch it. The best thing you can do with newspapers is to keep them sealed in plastic sleeves or bags, laid flat. Don't store them folded in half across the middle. They will eventually become stiff, and it's hard to turn pages with that extra crease. Magazines and books should also be kept in plastic sleeves or bags. *Never* store paper in damp or wet places!

FRAMING POSTERS, PRINTS, AND OTHER GRAPHICS

Always use acid-free board for the mat and the back board. The print or poster should not be attached to the back board at all if you are framing it to the edges. If you want to use a mat, the print should be carefully attached to the back board with two hinges of acid-free cloth tape (available in art supply stores). Or use a tiny amount of wheat-paste glue (sold in frame shops) in each of the top two corners. It is not a good idea to blindly trust your local frame shop with your prints and posters. Many of them use a spray glue and stick the piece to the back board. (The value of a dry mounted poster is destroyed the instant it hits the glue.) Even if you find someone to do the job properly with acid-free board, make sure the framer doesn't leave heavy pencil lines on the underside of the mat. These will transfer to a print.

Many dealers who sell posters will shrinkwrap them for sale. This protects them from damage before they are sold, and it's a good way to display them. However, it's not good to leave posters shrinkwrapped for long. The back board is usually foam-core, which is not quite acid-free, and the shrink-film will deteriorate, too.

Never hang anything where it will be faded by the sun. If you have much more than you can possibly hang up, the best storage for posters and prints is in a print file—a metal file cabinet with long narrow drawers used in art supply stores for storing paper. You can use an artist's portfolio if you put a sheet of acid-free mat board on either side of your collection to protect it. Or, you can get two sheets of acid-free mat board and sandwich your treasures between them. Don't use plain brown corrugated cardboard! It will eventually ruin your posters because of its high acid content.

TEXTILES

Like paper, textiles should not be stored in damp places. For long-term storage, a cedar chest will keep out moisture and any multilegged creatures who want to make their home in your collection. If you keep clothing on hangers, use the padded kind, or thick plastic. Never use wire hangers.

One type of fabric which was new in the late 1960s has a tendency to self-destruct! Bonded polyester has a foam-like backing which deteriorates into dry crumbs, and then the backing falls off. One person told me that this condition is caused by dry cleaning. However I have a piece of fabric that was never used, never worn, and never cleaned, that has almost completely come apart leaving behind vast quantities of red crumbs. I can just peel the whole back off and hopefully save the front fabric, but an item of clothing might be more difficult. If you have a piece that is deteriorating, put it away and don't wear it. It will last a little longer. If you are considering a purchase, check for crumbs. Unfortunately a number of good designs were made of this material.

GLASS AND POTTERY

Never put anything in the dishwasher. Even the best dishwasher will scratch your collectibles. You and a sponge are the best dishwashers, along with a mild soap. Don't get over-enthusiastic about scrubbing your Peter Max dishes. And *no* steel wool pot scrubbers on the enamel cookware!

OTHER ITEMS

It's best to display small objects such as toys in a glass- enclosed display case or cabinet. This will protect them from moisture, dust, children, pets, and all but the most determined of insects. Storage in cardboard boxes is okay, as long as you don't let paper collectibles, or any original boxes, rest directly against the cardboard box.

Books, Magazines and Newspapers

Books, magazines, and newspapers from the 1960s and 1970s are great for reference, besides being collectible in themselves. If you weren't there, they give you a better social view of life in the psychedelic era. (And even if you were there!) They are also good sources of information about psychedelic collectibles.

In this chapter, you will find the out-of-print, collectible books that were printed during the period on the subjects of psychedelic art, styles, politics, fashions, music, and pop culture. (Books that are presently in print are listed under "References.")

Magazines of the psychedelic era can be very informative to collectors. *Life* and *Look* magazines have many good articles and photographs on a variety of subjects pertaining to the era. Magazines like *TV Guide* or *Vogue* will interest more specialized collectors. And, a pile of *Mad* magazines is a lot of fun, as well as a "bass-ackward" reference of the time!

As for old newspapers, "yesterday's news" can be pretty interesting sometimes. In the psychedelic era, there were quite a few really good underground newspapers. The most collectible is the *San Francisco Oracle*. The famous San Francisco music poster artists contributed some great graphics to that paper, most of which were not printed anywhere else. That is unfortunate, because with time, the newspaper changes color and gets darker, dulling the originally bright colors.

You may notice that there aren't any general newspapers listed here. The establishment newspapers of the time usually didn't look favorably on psychedelia, hippies, protesting, rock music, or much of anything! The establishment news didn't really relate to the lives of a lot of people. Many were turned off by what they felt were inaccuracies and outright propaganda. (Try reading an establishment newspaper's account of events like the Chicago Democratic Convention, or *any* protest.) So there was a need for the underground press. The underground newspapers reveal more about what a large segment of the people were interested in, and their concerns. But they added their own slant to the news, too.

An important thing to keep in mind when reading *anything*, whether it is the collectibles in this chapter, or today's newspaper, is that the opinion of the writer is always present. It may be blatant, exalting their view while blasting the other; inaccurate reporting of facts and figures; or fairly subtle, using a word or phrase to influence opinions when portraying one item or another. News is supposed to be reporting the facts, and allowing the reader to form an opinion about them.

Collecting Hints

 Although hard to preserve, (see Keeping Your Collection in Good Shape in the Introduction), awkward to display, and sometimes even hard to handle without damaging, the written material from the psychedelic era can be very interesting. It gives different points of view in stories and graphics that represent the popular culture of the psychedelic period the best—straight from the people. Look for those issues reporting major events.

There are no reprints of any of this material. Although personally, I wouldn't mind if someone would reprint the *San Francisco Oracle* on *good quality paper!*

Books

Figure 1–1. The Great Poster Trip–Eureka. © *1968, edited by Cummings G. Walker. Coyne & Blanchard.* **$20–$30.**

Figure 1–2. Prop Art, © 1972, by Gary Yanker. Darien House, NY. **$30–$40.**

Figure 1–4. Mouse & Kelley, © 1979, Dell Publishing, NY, NY. **$15–$20.**

Figure 1–3. Psychedelic Art, © 1968, by Robert E. L. Masters & Jean Houston. A Ballance House Book, Grove Press, NY. **$40–$60.**

Figure 1–5. Man From Utopia, © 1972, by Rick Griffin. (Private printing) printed by Calitho, San Francisco, CA. **$15–$25.**

Figure 1–6. Get On Down (a decade of Rock and Roll Posters), © 1977, edited by Mick Farren. Futura Publications and Dempsey & Squires, Great Britain. **$25–$35.**

Figure 1–7. High Tide, © 1972, by Brad Johannsen with Bob Brockway and Karen Ghen. Harmony Books/Crown Publishers, NY. **$25.**

Figure 1–8. 1. Steal This Book, © 1971, by Abbie Hoffman. Pirate Editions, NY. **$15–$20.** 2. Do It! © 1970, by Jerry Rubin. Ballantine Books, NY. **$10–$15.**

Figure 1–9. Defiance #1 and Defiance #2, © 1970 & 1971, edited by Dotson Rader. Paperback Library. **$8–$15** each.

Figure 1–10. The Hippie Papers, © 1968, edited by Jerry Hopkins. Signet Books, NY. **$15.**

Figure 1-11. Top: 1. American Pop, © 1969, by David Dachs. Scholastic Book Services, NY. **$10.** 2. Pop Rock Lyrics, © 1969, by Jerry L. Walker. Scholastic Book Services, NY. **$10.** 3. The Pop Makers, © 1966, by Caroline Silver. Scholastic Book Services, NY. **$10.** Bottom: 1. TV '70, © 1969, by Peggy Hudson. Scholastic Book Services, NY. **$10.** 2. The Hippie Scene, © 1968, by Carolyn Barnes. Scholastic Book Services, NY. **$15.** 3. Hair Today . . . and Gone Tomorrow! © 1969, by Betty Wason. Scholastic Book Services, NY. **$5.**

Figure 1-13. All Stars (contains a selection of pieces from most psychedelic and underground comics). Published by San Francisco Comic Book Co. **$50.**

Figure 1-12. The Black Panthers Speak, © 1970, edited by Philip S. Foner. J.B. Lippincott Company, Phila., PA. **$15.**

Figure 1-14. As Time Goes By, © 1973, by Derek Taylor. Straight Arrow Books, San Francisco, CA. **$15.**

Figure 1–15. Lizard Zen, © 1973, by Vaughn Bodē. Published by T.K. II, Cambridge, MA. **$30.**

Figure 1–18. Mad Magazines, 1965–1974. (A "Mad" look at the period); **$5–$15** each.

Magazines

Figure 1–16. Avant Garde, 1960s. **$18–$50** each.

Figure 1–19. Charlie magazine, 1971. **$10.**

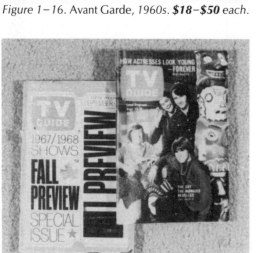

Figure 1–17. TV Guides, 1965–1974. **$5–$50** each (depending on the content).

Figure 1–20. Life magazines, 1965–1972. (Contained a variety of relevant articles); **$5–$35** each, (depending on the content).

Underground Comics

Figure 1–21. Teenset, 1960s. **$8–$15** each.

Figure 1–23. Legion of Charlies, 1971 (1st printing). Greg Irons, artist (did posters for concerts). Last Gasp Ecor Funnies, Berkeley, CA; **$15.**

Figure 1–22. Freak Out USA, February, 1967. **$15.**

Figure 1–24. Deviant Slice, 1972 (1st printing). Greg Irons, artist (did posters for concerts). The Print Mint, Berkeley, CA; **$10.**

Figure 1–25. Mr. Natural *No. 2, 1971. R. Crumb, artist. San Francisco Comicbook Co., S.F.;* **$10.**

Figure 1–27. The Forty Year Old Hippie, *No. 2, 1979. Ted Richards, artist. The Rip Off Press, Inc. S.F., CA;* **$5.**

Figure 1–26. Mickey Rat *No. 1, 1972. Robert Armstrong, artist. Los Angeles Comic Book Co.;* **$25.** Mickey Rat *No. 2, 1972.* **$8.**

Figure 1–28. Yellow Dog. *Vol. II No. 5. The Print Mint, Berkeley, CA;* **$10.**

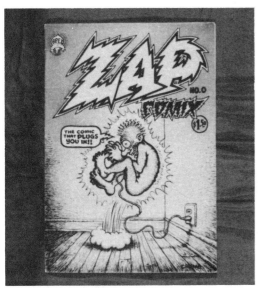

Figure 1–29. Zam, 1974. S. Clay Wilson, Rick Griffin, Victor Moscoso, R. Williams, R. Crumb, Gilbert Shelton, Spain Rodrigues artists. **$8–$15.**

Figure 1–31. San Francisco Oracle. **$35–$75** *each.*

The famous San Francisco poster artists contributed great graphics to this paper. The better the graphics, the more expensive the paper.

Newspapers

Figure 1–30. Zap No. 0 (not the 1st Zap). The Print Mint, Berkeley, CA; **$40.**

Figure 1–32. Other Scenes, 1968 *(underground newspaper).* **$10–$15.**

13

Figure 1–33. The East Village Other, NY. **$10–$15** each.

Figure 1–35. The Chicago Seed, Corpus, EST East, the Mountain Free Press, *and* Astral Projection *(underground newspapers).* **$10–$15** each.

Figure 1–34. Changes, Vol. 1, No. 1, 1969 (music newspaper). **$40–$60.**

Figure 1–36. The East Village Other, NY. Issues with art, by R. Crumb, 1968; and by John Thompson, poster artist, 1967. **$20** each.

Figure 1–37. Rat (New York underground paper), 1968. **$10–$15** each.

Figure 1–38. Screw, 1968 (sex newspaper).
$25–$30 *with John and Yoko on cover,* ***$5–$10***
each, other issues.

    Occasionally had relevant psychedelic articles.

Figure 1–39. Rolling Stone, 1968 (music paper).
$50–$75, *early issues.*

    This one's autographed, so it's value is ***$100.***

Clothing

A huge variety of clothing was created during the psychedelic era. People had more to choose from than ever before, ranging from the boring to the bizarre.

Leading the clothing industry were the designers, the gurus of fashion. Their clothing was, and still is, very expensive. In the '60s the look was "mod." It seems as if they were trying to "out-mod" each other with "space-age" designs and all kinds of odd materials. New technology gave them plastics, vinyl, "non-woven fabric" (otherwise known as paper), polyester, metallic fabrics, etc. It was an era of experimentation.

Mod styles began much earlier than we usually imagine. The space-age mod look began around 1964. The hard bright colors, contrasts of black and white, and geometric designs of pop art were translated into clothing. But, it takes a while for new styles to filter down to the general public. The mod-style clothing that people could buy at department stores was less expensive and usually toned down in style.

Of the established designers, Emilio

Pucci could be considered the most psychedelic, with his vibrantly colorful art nouveau designs. I think Pucci clothing is a pretty good buy right now, and I expect to see it rise in price.

At the same time, there was the hippie style, or anti-style. Doing your own thing. No plastics for them—only natural materials like cotton and leather. Ethnic styles were popular, with imports from India, the Philippines. South America, and Africa. Hippies didn't want the establishment's clothing designers, either. And old clothing was salvaged from thrift shops. Today's antique and vintage clothing was first "discovered" by hippies interested in the flamboyant and romantic Victorian, Edwardian, and Flapper era styles. Around 1969–1970, hippie fashions became the youth-oriented styles made by establishment manufacturers. The American manufacturers and stores were not willing to lose all the young people's business to the imports.

We shouldn't forget about the hippie clothing-crafts that they made themselves. They experimented with tie-die and batik. Embroidery, beadwork, patchwork, crochet, and paint were used to embellish and personalize their denim jeans, jackets, and vests. These hand-done pieces of folk art are very rare.

American Indian styles and long, long fringes, either on leather or cloth with lots of beadwork were also popular around 1968 to 1971. The American flag also became a motif for clothing, especially since wearing it annoyed the establishment. Men's ties went wild starting in 1967: Wide, with paisleys and psychedelic patterns. For the first time in a few centuries, men wore exciting and colorful clothes, even if it was only a splashy tie with a grey suit.

The most desirable fashions of the era are the creations of the psychedelic clothing boutiques. These were the places where the rock musicians shopped (and other cool people, too). Representations of this stylish stuff can be found in old photographs of the Who, Beatles, Rolling Stones, Jimi Hendrix, The Byrds, Strawberry Alarm Clock, Sly and the Family Stone, and many other music personalities of the time. Look for goodies from "Granny Takes a Trip" of New York and London, "Paraphernalia." "Bouncing Bertha's Banana Blanket," "Alkasura Clothing Ltd." of London, Mary Quant's "Bazaar" in England (she invented the mini), "Biba" (also of England), and boots and shoes from "Terry de Haviland." But labels aren't everything. Anything really outrageous looking is great, even if you don't know who made it. So far, the major auction houses have sold this type of clothing, but only with a celebrity provenance. Elton John's or Keith Richard's clothing is definitely more valuable than similar items with no celebrity status.

Hair is definitely not a collectible in itself. (Well, you could collect wigs and photographs, I guess). Part of the fashion of the time for both men and women, was long hair. A hippie's long hair was a symbol of freedom from the regimented style of their fathers and the fake, hair-sprayed styles of their mothers. It was also a symbol of pacifism. Short hair had been invented in ancient times for the military, so that nobody could grab a person by the hair in battle. Therefore: Long-Hairs don't fight.

With the mod clothing of 1966 to 1968, the style for hair on women was a short "bob" such as Twiggy wore. In the 1920s, short hair for women was a symbol of freedom and the "modern" liberated woman. It was the same in the earlier 1960s—a symbol for the modern woman. Then around 1968, fashion changed to long, straight hair for women. This fad induced many of those with curls to try to flatten their hair. (Incidentally, ironing your hair doesn't work.)

Figure 2-2. Dress, crochet, circa 1969. "100% wool, Hand made in Hong Kong." Cream, $20-$30.

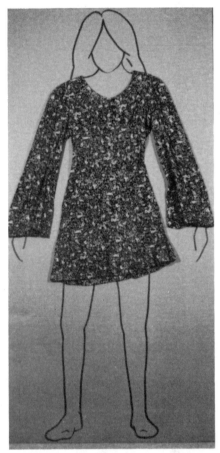

Figure 2-3. Mini dress, cotton, circa 1969-70 (see color section). Blue/orange/pink/yellow/green, $35.

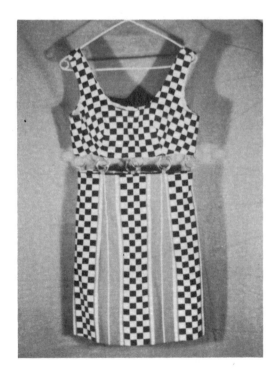

Figure 2-1. Mini dress, polyester with Lucite circles, circa 1968. "Corner One." White/black/red, $50-$75.

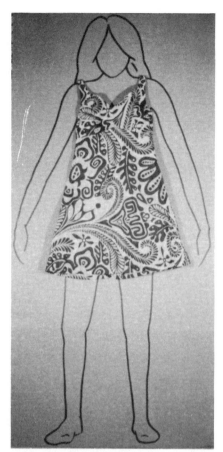

*Figure 2–4. Dress, Maxi-length, cotton, circa 1970. Blue/pink/purple/yellow/orange/white, **$20–$30.***

*Figure 2–5. Sun Dress, cotton, circa 1968. "Bobbie Brooks, Made in USA." White/blue/orange, **$20.***

*Figure 2–6. Paper Dress, circa 1969 "Sleeveless MuuMuu, Hallmark, Kansas City, MO." Various, (package) $14\frac{1}{8}'' \times 9\frac{3}{4}''$. **$20.***

*Figure 2–7. Dress, cotton, circa 1970–72. "Kaiser, 100% cotton, Made in Pakistan." Tan/lavender/ pink/blue, **$35.***

*Figure 2–8. Dress (can also be worn over pants), cotton, circa 1969. "Morgan of London." Red/ blue/beige/gold, **$45.***

*Figure 2–9. Paper Dress, circa 1969. "Flower Fantasy Hallmark, Kansas City, MO." Pink/yellow/ green/white, **$15–$20.***

Figure 2–10. Paper Dress, circa 1968. "The Souper Dress." White/red/black/gold, **$250.**

Figure 2–11. Mini skirt, velvet, circa 1968. "Emilio Pucci, Made for Saks Fifth Ave., Made in Italy." Black/peacock blues/greens, **$50–$75.**

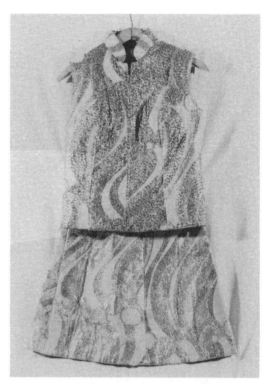

Figure 2–12. Skirt and sleeveless jacket, metallic and sequined, circa 1969. Green/gold/purple, **$65.**

Figure 2–13. Nehru Jacket, circa 1965–67. Blue with purple buttons, **$35–$50.**

Figure 2–14. Jacket, velvet, with beads and rhinestones, circa 1969. "Granny Takes a Trip." Black, **$75–$100.**

Figure 2–15. Jacket, circa 1970. "Granny Takes a Trip." Black with pink and green sequins, **$50–$60.**

Figure 2–16. Jacket, lurex (stretchy), circa 1969. "Granny Takes a Trip." Metallic silver, **$50–$75.**

Figure 2–17. Jacket, Snake skin, circa 1970. "Ruskin." Beige/brown, **$200.**

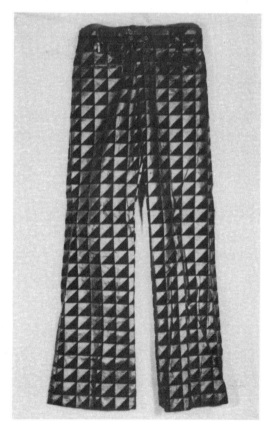

Figure 2–18. Pants, vinyl and velvet, circa 1968–70. Black, **$30–$50.**

Figure 2-19. Jeans, denim, circa 1968-70. Red/white/blue/gold, **$35-$40.**

Figure 2-20. Shirt, circa 1969. (Bought in London.) Bright green, **$25.**

Figure 2-21. Man's sport coat, circa 1969. "Original from Brad Whitney, California." White/black/tan/rust/olive green, **$60-$75.**

Figure 2-22. Shirt, circa 1970-73. "Expressions by Campus." Black, **$35-$40.**

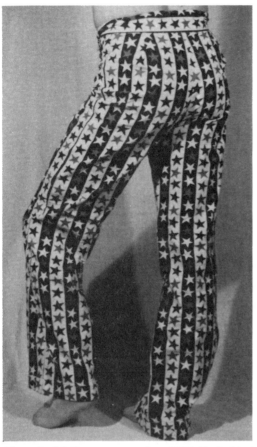

Figure 2–23. Pants, cotton, circa 1969. Red/white/blue, **$45.**

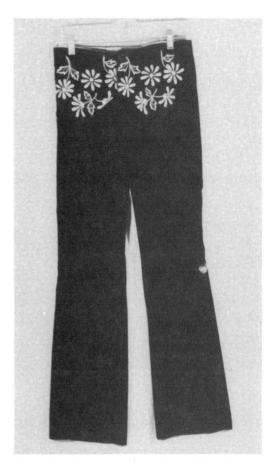

Figure 2–25. Pants, velvet, circa 1969. "Granny Takes a Trip." Green/black/white flowers, **$35–$50.**

Figure 2–24. Vest, suede, circa 1968. "Neiman-Marcus." Brown, **$35–$50.**

Figure 2–26. Shirt, circa 1967–68. "Golden Fleetline." Black/white, **$25–$35.**

Figure 2–27. Pants, satin, circa 1969. "Alkasura Clothing Limited, London." Brown, $35–$45.

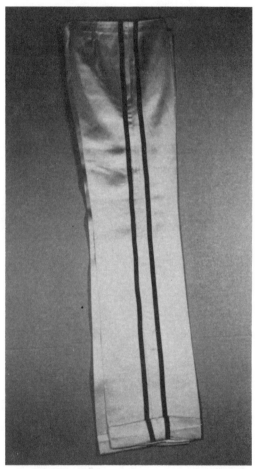

Figure 2–28. Pants, satin, circa 1969. "Alkasura Clothing Limited, London." Orange/black side stripe, $40–$50.

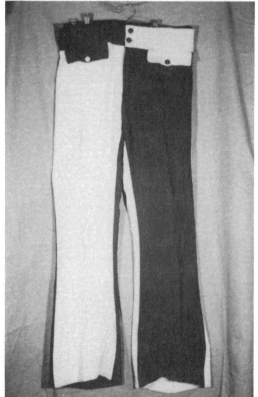

Figure 2–29. Pants, polyester, circa 1968–70. Purple/white, $35–$45.

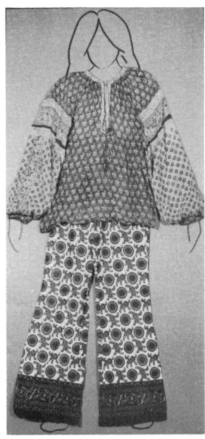

Figure 2–30. Top, polyester, circa 1967 (may have had a matching skirt). "carlye." Red/white, **$15.** Pants, advertising Coke, cotton, circa 1971. Red/white, **$45.**

Figure 2–32. Top, see-through printed cotton, circa 1969–72. (Probably made in India.) Purple/cream/blue, **$20.** Pants, printed cotton hip-hugger bell-bottoms, circa 1969. Blue/white, **$35.**

Figure 2–31. Shirt, dacron polyester and cotton, circa 1970. "Majesty." Brown/white, **$25–$30.**

*Figure 2–33. Shirt, cotton, circa 1970. White/red/maroon/blue/yellow/green, **$15–$25.***

*Figure 2–35. Shirt, cotton, circa 1970. "The Dashiki." Blue/red/gold/brown, **$20–$25.***

*Figure 2–34. Shirt, circa 1970–72. "Now Look by Grants." Beige/blue/red/brown, **$15–$20.***

*Figure 2–36. Shirt, circa 1969. "Van Heusen." Yellow/red, **$20.***

Figure 2-37. Shirt, moire silk, circa 1968-70. "Monzini Collection." Black, **$40-$60.**

Figure 2-40. Sleeveless shell, wool with large sequins, circa 1967. "Hand Beaded in Hong Kong." Black/white, **$50.**

Figure 2-38. Shirt, circa 1968-69. "Artvogue of California." Multicolor, **$25-$30.**

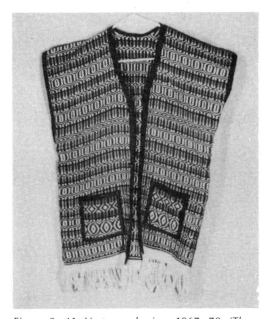

Figure 2-41. Vest, wool, circa 1967-70. (These were handwoven in South America.) White/black/red/blue, **$15-$20.**

Figure 2-39. Top, rayon, circa 1969. "Balouch, Made in Afghanistan, 100% rayon, Dry clean, Hollywood, CA." Pink, **$25-$30.**

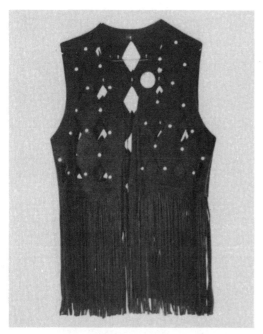

Figure 2–42. Vest, suede, circa 1969–70. Black with silver metal studs, **$35–$45.**

Figure 2–43. Vest, vinyl, circa 1970. "London Mod." Black/red stitching/white buttons, **$35.**

Figure 2–44. Lounging Outfit, circa 1968. Black/white, **$30.**

Figure 2–45. Boots, circa 1968–70. 1. Leather, wood heels. "Andy's Heel Bar", London (Custom Made). Metallic copper/green/black, **$40.** 2. Vinyl. Black, **$35.**

Figure 2-46. Raincoat, vinyl, circa 1968. "Lilli Ann, Paris/San Francisco." Black/white, **$65-$85.** Rain Hat, vinyl, circa 1967. "Made in the British Crown Colony of Hong Kong." Black/white, **$15-$20.**

Figure 2-48. Boots, vinyl foot, cloth top, circa 1969-71. Black with multicolored embroidery, **$35.**

Figure 2-49. Go-go boots, circa 1968. Metallic gold, **$40.**

Figure 2-47. Boots, Stretch-fabric, circa 1968-70. Red/blue/white, **$75-$125.**

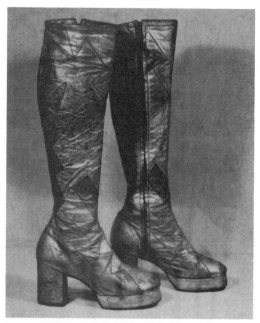

Figure 2−50. Boots, leather, circa 1968−70. "Terry de Haviland, London." Metallic silver/red/blue, **$100.**

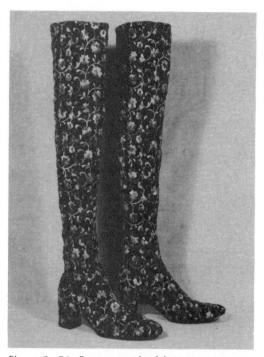

Figure 2−51. Boots, stretchy fabric (goes up past the knees), circa 1968 (see color section). "Goloboots." Black with multicolored embroidered floral design, **$100.**

Figure 2−52. Boots, snake skin, circa 1969−70. "Terry de Haviland." Red, **$75−$125.**

Figure 2−53. Shoes. 1. Leather, circa 1967−68. "Lujano, Hand made in Italy." Purple, **$35−$40.** 2. Velvet, circa 1970−72. "Thom McAn." Red, **$20.**

Figure 2−54. Shoes, cloth, circa 1970. "Lang Padrilles, Made in Florence, Italy." Pale blue/grey, **$20.**

*Figure 2–55. Shoes, snake skin, circa 1972–73. "Made by Lugran for The Common Market. Made in Spain." Red/brown, **$50.***

*Figure 2–56. Shoes, leather and snake skin, circa 1970. "Regal." Black with natural (brown) snake, **$25–$35.***

Jewelry and Accessories

3

Much of the jewelry of the psychedelic period was more than just decoration. It was a political or personal statement of the wearer. Peace, Ecology, Equality of races and sexes, and religious, moral and ideological ideas were made into cast metal. Love beads were a political statement. And if you had no other opinions, you could wear your astrological sign. With your choice in jewelry, you could display your thoughts and beliefs in public at all times. It was a great way to advertise.

Mod jewelry was usually bright, colorful, and often exaggerated in form. *Big* jewelry was in. Rings so large that they would inhibit movement, big flower pins, wide watches, broad ties and belts.

Hippie craftspeople created their own designs in jewelry. Their products varied with their individual abilities. Some made really awful collage pieces, some made spectacular ones. Some worked in silver and turquoise, in the

American Indian tradition, so well that it is sometimes hard to tell the difference between their work and real Indian jewelry. A few made very sophisticated creations using gold and gem stones. I recently saw a beautiful gold roach clip pendant of abstract form, that was made by a man who doesn't look like a hippie craftsman anymore! For some hippies, crafts were a good way of making money without selling out to the establishment.

There are some particularly unusual items with earlier roots that were popular during the psychedelic period. Slave bracelets, a bracelet connected by chains to one or more rings on the same hand; and ankle bracelets were a modern version of ancient fashion. Chokers were popular in the late nineteenth century, and headbands were traditional American Indian fashion. Other peculiar items were puzzle rings, often used to entertain the wearer in a boring class; and mood rings of the early 1970s, a precursor to the digital thermometer! The theory behind mood rings was that a tense person has cool hands, and as a person relaxes his hands grow warmer. The theory continued that someone in love had really warm hands. The stone in a mood ring changed color in direct relation to the warmth of the hand it graced. The rings weren't always accurate, but people had fun with them.

Collecting Hints

 So far, none of these items has been reproduced. Ankh jewelry has been remade recently, but it is different from the originals. (See Collecting Hints under "Peace Symbols".) The interest in making reproductions has not yet expanded to include much more than peace symbols. Presently, jewelry is inexpensive, and it's a good buy. It is likely to escalate in price. (You are liable to pay more for *new* jewelry than for originals right now!) Look for unusual items for your collection. *Note:* Peace symbol items are in chapter 4, Smilie jewelry is in chapter 13, and Peter Max jewelry and accessories are in chapter 11.

Figure 3–1. Necklaces. 1. Pewter, "War is not healthy for children and other living things"; **$15.** *2. Pewter, "Peace/Love";* **$10.** *3. Pewter, "Love—War is not good";* **$10.**

Figure 3–2. Necklaces. 1. Pewter, "Peace"; **$8–$10.** *2. Pewter, "Love";* **$8–$10.**

Figure 3–3. Necklaces. 1. Pewter, "Peace"; **$5–$10.** 2. Pewter, "Love"; **$5–$10.**

Figure 3–4. Necklaces. 1. Pewter, "I am a friend of the earth"; **$5–$10.** 2. Pewter, "Live Life"; **$5–$10.**

Figure 3–5. Necklaces. 1. Pewter, "Too much sex makes your eye . . ."; **$5–$8.** 2. Pewter, male/female; **$5–$8.**

Figure 3–6. Necklace (mod). Red enamel on gold colored metal; 17" long; **$15–$25.**

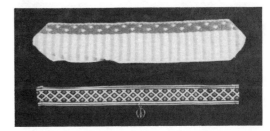

Figure 3–7. Chokers, circa 1970. Top: Cloth. White/blue/red; **$8–$10.** Bottom: Cloth with metal peace dangle. White/green/black/yellow; **$8–$10.**

Figure 3–8. Necklace, glass seed beads, circa 1970. Red/white/blue; 19" long; **$20–$30.**

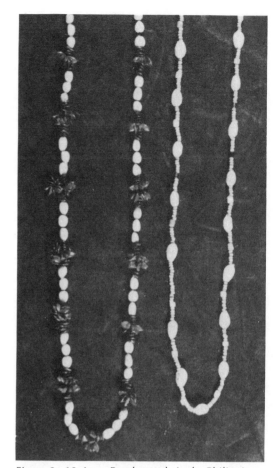

Figure 3–10. Love Beads, made in the Philippines, circa 1969. 1. Natural seeds. Brown/white; **$10.** 2. Wood beads with multicolored glass beads. **$10.**

Figure 3–9. Necklaces, low-grade silver, circa 1969–70. Made in India. 1. **$15–$20.** 2. **$20–$25.**

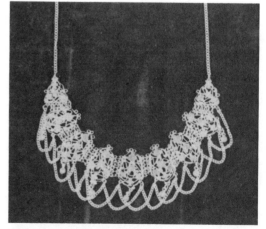

Figure 3–11. Choker, low-grade silver, circa 1970. Made in India. **$15–$20.**

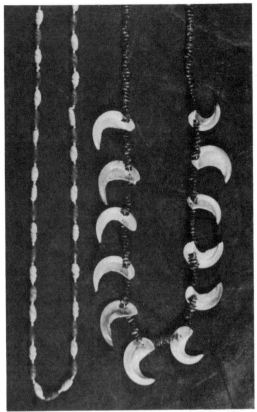

Figure 3–12. Love Beads, made in the Philippines, circa 1969. 1. Brown and black clay beads with green glass seed beads. 19" long; $5–$10. 2. Natural nuts and seeds. Brown; 17" long; $8–$10.

Figure 3–13. Earrings. 1. Gold-colored metal; $10. 2. Gold-colored metal/blue enamel; $10.

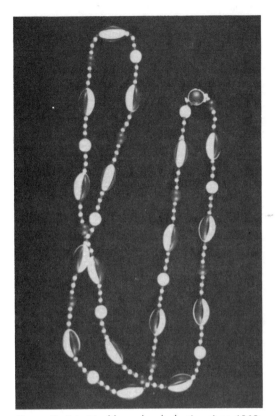

Figure 3–14. Necklace, hard plastic, circa 1969. "Hong Kong." Bright pink/turquoise; 27" long; $15–$20.

Figure 3–15. Earrings, vinyl, circa 1968. White/pink/green; $5–$10.

Figure 3–16. Love Pin, enamel on thin metal, cardboard back, circa 1972. Robert Indiana Design. Red/blue/green; 1½"; $15–$25.

*Figure 3–17. Necklace, low-grade silver wire, circa 1969. Made in India. **$10–$15.***

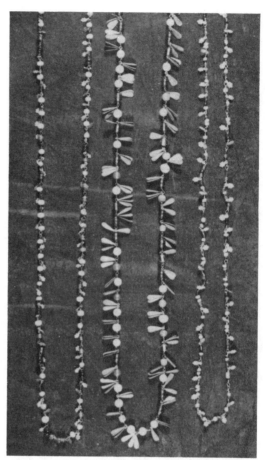

*Figure 3–19. Love Beads, Multicolored glass beads and brass, circa 1969–71. 1. 20" long; **$10.** 2. 30" long; **$25.** 3. 22" long; **$10.***

*Figure 3–20. Love double ring, cast metal, circa 1972. Gold-colored metal/black; $1\frac{1}{2}$"; **$15.***

*Figure 3–18. Flower pins, enameled metal, circa 1967–68. Brightly colored; **$10–$25** each.*

Large pins of this type are preferable to small ones.

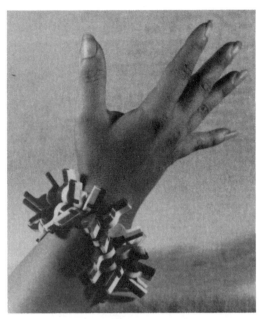

Figure 3–21. Bracelet, plastic whistles on elastic. Green/white; **$20–$30.**

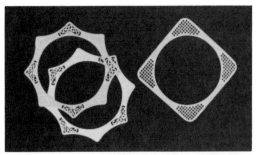

Figure 3–23. Bracelets, cast metal. Enameled various flourescent colors; **$5** each.

Figure 3–24. Medallion, Martin Luther King memorial. Pewter; **$10–$15.**

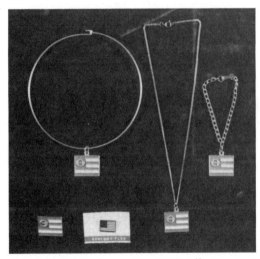

Figure 3–25. Ecology, circa 1972 (all are green/white/gold). Top row: 1. Choker, **$15.** 2. Necklace, **$15.** 3. Bracelet, **$12.** Bottom row: 1. Pin, **$15.** 2. Tie tack, **$10.**

On the back of the original card there is a printed explanation: "Greek letter, theta, warning of death, symbolizes the threat to earth and its atmosphere. Green stripes are for unspoiled land, white for pure air."

Figure 3–22. Slave bracelet, circa 1968–69. Gold-colored metal and amber glass; **$25–$30.**

Figure 3–26. Ankh jewelry (Ancient Egyptian Life Symbol). Top row: 1. Ring, gold-colored/white enamel; $10. 2. Ring, gold-colored; $8. 3. Ring, sterling, made in Mexico; $15–$20. 4. Ring, pewter; $15. Bottom row: 1. Earrings, gold-colored/blue enamel; $10. 2. Earrings, gold-colored/multi-color beads; $15. 3. Earrings, gold-colored/red enamel; $10.

Figure 3–27. Sunglasses, plastic, circa 1968–70. 1. Foster Grant; pink/grey. 2. Foster Grant; white. 3. White/black. 4. Orange/black; $10–$20 each.

Figure 3–28. Sunglasses, metal frame, glass, circa 1968. Frame silver: glass green; $20–$25.

Figure 3–29. Sunglasses, metal frame, glass, circa 1968. Frame gold; glass rose-color; $20–$25.

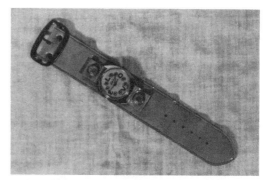

Figure 3–30. Watch, vinyl and metal, circa 1970. "Lucerne Watch Co." Green/brass; $35.

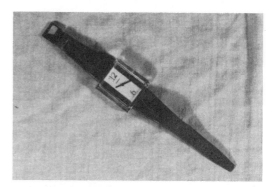

Figure 3–31. Watch, vinyl and lucite, circa 1968. "Endura." Blue band; blue/white/clear lucite watch; $45–$65.

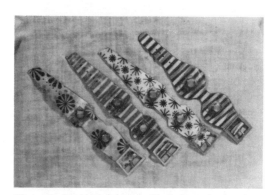

Figure 3–32. Watch bands, Vari-view plastic, circa 1969. Various color combinations, $10–$15 each.

Figure 3–33. Hair Barrettes, leather, circa 1970. 1. Brown; **$5–$10.** 2. Pink/purple; **$5.**

Figure 3–34. Headbands, circa 1970. 1. Cloth with elastic band; blue/white; **$10.** 2. Cloth with vinyl backing and elastic. Red/yellow/pink/white/green/black; **$5.**

Figure 3–35. Patches, cloth. Top row: 1. Black/white/red; 3"; **$5.** 2. White/red/blue; 3"; **$5.** 3. Pink/purple; 3"; **$4.** 4. Blue/white/pink; 3"; **$8–$10.** Middle row: 1. Blue/white/green; $3\frac{1}{8}$"; **$5.** 2. Blue/white/red; $2\frac{3}{4}$"; **$4.** 3. Black/pink/yellow; $3\frac{1}{8}$"; **$5–$8.** 4. Blue/gold; 3"; **$4.** Bottom row: 1. White/blue; 3"; **$4.** 2. White/blue/red/gold; $4\frac{1}{4}$"; **$4.** 3. Blue/white/black; $3\frac{1}{8}$"; **$3.** 4. Blue/white/gold/red; 3"; **$3.** 5. Red/white; $2\frac{3}{4}$"; **$4.**

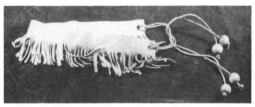

Figure 3–36. Fringed belt, leather with wood beads, circa 1969. Purple/cream; **$10.**

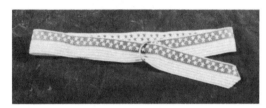

Figure 3–37. Belt, cloth, circa 1970. White/blue/red; **$15–$20.**

Figure 3–38. Belt, cast metal hands with leather, circa 1969. Gold hands, black leather; **$15–$20.**

Figure 3–39. Belt, cloth and leather, circa 1968. Green/light green/orange/gold; **$10.**

Figure 3–40. Belts Top: *Leather with wood beads, circa 1969. Purple/cream;* **$10.** *Middle: Woven cloth, circa 1970–72. Multicolor;* **$5–$10.** *Bottom: Vinyl, circa 1967–68. Red;* **$10.**

Figure 3–41. Gloves. Cloth and vinyl, circa 1966–67 (see color section). "Made in Western Germany." Black/white; $20.

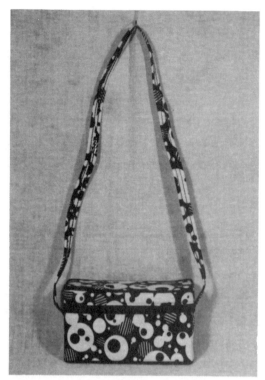

Figure 3–43. Shoulder Bag, vinyl, circa 1969. Black/white; $30–$40.

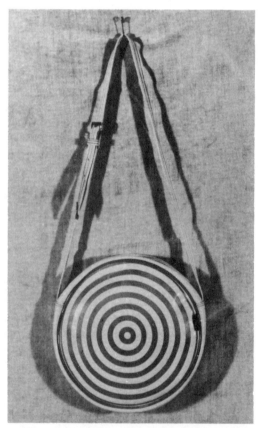

Figure 3–42. Shoulder Bag, vinyl, circa 1967–68. Designer: Fiorucci. White/orange; $40–$65.

Figure 3–44. Scarf, silk, circa 1969–71. "Shahzadi Blockprint, India." Light green/dark green; 7'8" long; $30–$40.

Figure 3–47. Scarf, circa 1971. Yellow/orange/pink/green/white/blue; **$10–$15.**

Figure 3–45. Shoulder Bag, leather, circa 1969–70 (see color section). Blue/white/red; **$40–$60.**

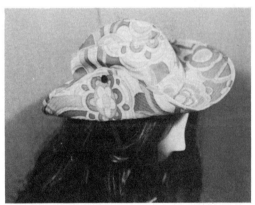

Figure 3–48. Hat, cotton, circa 1970. "Made in Hong Kong." Blue/pink/orange/olive/yellow; **$35–$45.**

Figure 3–46. Hat, cotton, circa 1967. "Ruth Clarage, Hand Printed Original, Montego Bay, Ocho Rios, Kingston." Teal blue/olive green; **$20.**

Figure 3–49. Ties, circa 1969. "Radium, Pure silk, Made in India." 1. Turquoise/green/blue/gold. 2. Turquoise/green/black/peach/pale green. *$10–$15* each.

Figure 3–51. Tie, silk, circa 1969. "Christian Dior, Paris." Black/purple/gold/pink/olive/chartreuse; *$20–$30.*

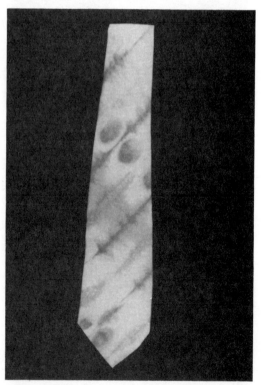

Figure 3–50. Tie, cotton, circa 1970. Tie-die, orange/yellow/white/tan; *$10–$15.*

Figure 3–52. Ties, circa 1968–70. "Emilio Pucci, Italy." 1. Brown/grey/black. 2. Blue/white/red. 3. White/blue/pink. 4. Various shades of purple/ brown/black/white. 5. Gold/greys/browns/black/ orange. *$25–$35* each.

Peace Symbols

Nobody seems to be quite sure of exactly where and when the circular peace symbol was invented. The most likely theory is that it came from a nuclear warning symbol. But I have also heard it was a broken cross, or (popular with political hawks) a symbol of the American Chicken, because of it's resemblance to a bird's footprint. Some of the earlier peace symbols were made without the bottom half of the center vertical line, which is like the nuclear warning symbol. One collector told me that the earliest peace symbol he's seen was from 1964—most date from 1968 to 1972.

The two-finger hand gesture is easily traced to the World War II "V for Victory." (When Winston Churchill did it, it was Victory, not Peace!) But then Victory meant the end of the war and therefore, Peace.

People who wore peace symbols were expressing their views on politics, the Vietnam war, war in general, and life as they saw it. Unfortunately, today some modern young people wear peace symbols just because they're "in," without considering what they really mean. In fairness, though, some of our youth do care about what the symbol represents. The reaction of their parents (who are the right age to remember the 1960s) is interesting. It ranges from enthusiasm to forbidding their kids to wear them.

Some people equate the peace symbol and hippies with drugs. I've heard of stores that have removed the new peace symbols from their stock for the same reason. But, in fact, the peace symbol just means peace—nothing more.

Collecting Hints

Figure 4–1. Jewelry Box, plastic, circa 1972. Black/silver; 4" × 6" × 2"; $30–$35.

Recently, peace symbols have been reproduced. New jewelry is not textured like most of the old pieces. New items are always round, flat, and shiny; none of the oval or teardrop shapes have been reproduced. Unfortunately, some new jewelry looks a lot like the period pieces so it may be hard to tell the difference. No leather, pewter, or beaded designs are being reproduced.

There is a new bracelet available, which was never made originally. It is styled like the Mexican sterling rings of the period. (A peace symbol, a line, a vertical row of three circles, a line, a peace symbol, and so on.) The new bracelet is hinged, with a dangling chain. Copies of the ring are being made also, but they are easily distinguished by a mold seam around the middle. It's not a very good casting. However, don't confuse these with the original copies, which may have the sterling mark, even though they are not silver.

Figure 4–2. Necklaces. 1. "Peace," gold-colored metal; $10. 2. Pewter (unusual shape); $20. 3. "Peace," pewter; $10–$15.

Figure 4–3. Necklaces. 1. "Love" peace symbol, cast nickel; $10–$15. 2. "Love" peace symbol, pewter-finished metal; $10–$15.

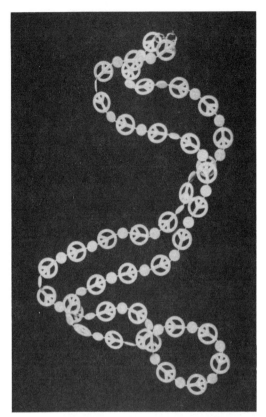

Figure 4–4. Necklace, plastic. Purple/pink (also comes in red/green, yellow/black, and blue/orange; **$20–$25.**

Figure 4–6. Dove/peace symbol, cast pewter; **$15.**

Figure 4–5. Choker, gold-colored metal (very thin). $15\frac{1}{2}$" long; **$15–$20.**

Figure 4–7. Necklaces. 1. Aluminum dog tags. Silver-colored with red peace symbol, blue dove; **$10–$15.** 2. "Peace" dove, silver-colored metal; **$10–$15.** 3. Aluminum dog tags. Silver-colored with red peace symbol, blue dove; **$10–$15.**

Figure 4–8. Necklaces. 1. Peace hand, pewter. **$15.** 2. "Peace," pewter. **$15.** 3. Woman power, pewter. **$15.**

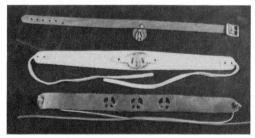

Figure 4–9. Chokers or head-bands. Top: Brown leather, gold-colored, metal peace symbol. **$5–$10.** Middle: Soft tan leather, silver-colored, metal peace symbol. **$8–$10.** Bottom: Soft brown leather, punched through design. **$5–$10.**

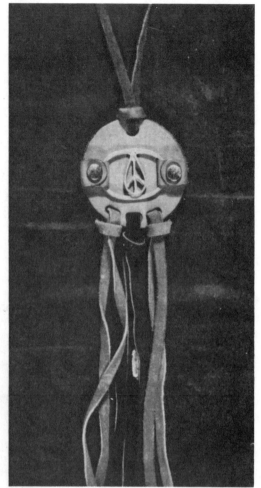

Figure 4–11. Necklaces, leather. 1. Red; **$10.** 2. Brown/brass studs; **$10–$15.**

Figure 4–10. Necklace, leather with long leather fringes. Brown circle with gold-colored peace symbol and studs, purple necklace, red and black fringes. 40" long; **$20.**

Can be used for a head band or tied at the knee.

Figure 4–12. Choker, cloth with gold-colored metal; **$15.**

Figure 4–13. Rings. Top row: 1. Copper; **$15.** 2. Pewter; **$15.** 3. Pewter; **$15.** 4. Copper; **$10.** Middle row: 1. Enameled metal; Red/white/blue; **$12.** 2. Silver-colored metal; **$6–$10.** 3. Pewter; **$8–$12.** 4. Pewter; **$10.** Bottom row: 1. Pewter; **$15.** 2. Gold-colored metal (heavy); **$15–$20.** 3. Gold-colored metal with blue enamel; **$6–$10.** 4. Leather with gold-colored metal; **$10.**

Figure 4–14. Pin, "peace" dove, silver-colored metal. **$20–$25.**

Pins are hard to find, necklaces are more common.

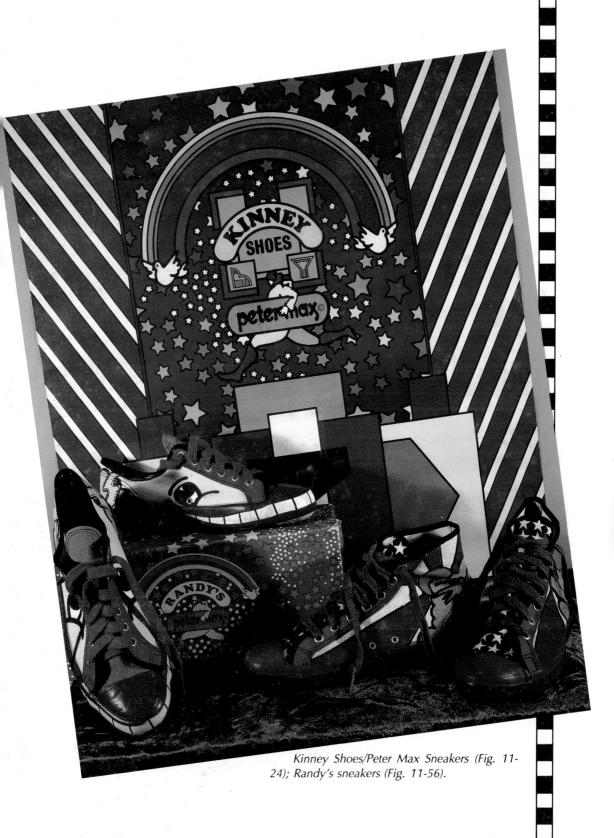

Kinney Shoes/Peter Max Sneakers (Fig. 11-24); Randy's sneakers (Fig. 11-56).

Chuck Berry/Sons of Champlin (see Fig. 9-23 for details).

Jimi Hendrix/John Mayall/Albert King (see Fig. 9-48 for details).

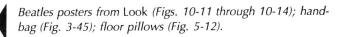

Beatles posters from Look (Figs. 10-11 through 10-14); hand-bag (Fig. 3-45); floor pillows (Fig. 5-12).

"Turn Off, Tune Out, Drop In" (see Fig. 12-2).

"Bring the Troops Home Now" (see Fig. 12-4).

Byrds/Moby Grape/Andrew Staples; Bill Graham production at Fillmore Auditorium.

New York City Center Anniversary, 1968 (Fig. 10-8); chrome floor lamp (Fig. 5-31); chrome upholstered chair (Fig. 5-8); chrome side table (Fig. 5-11); desk lamp (Fig. 5-26).

Molded plastic chair and table (Fig. 5-4); "Dove" poster (Fig. 11-19); curtains (Fig. 11-37); hand-blown glass bowl (Fig. 5-56).

Unused Woodstock poster, designed before location change (see Fig. 8-1 for details).

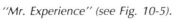

"Mr. Experience" (see Fig. 10-5).

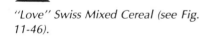

"Love" Swiss Mixed Cereal (see Fig. 11-46).

"Turn On Your Mind" (see Fig. 10-15).

Mini dress (Fig. 2-1); golo boots (Fig. 2-51).

Figure 4–15. Pin, cast silver-colored metal. marked "c.MV." Value unknown. (I've never seen another one of these!)

Figure 4–16. Watch band. Brown leather with red printed peace symbol and "peace;" gold-colored buckle. **$8–$12.**

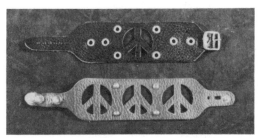

Figure 4–17. Wrist bands, leather. Top: Black/brass studs; **$5–$10.** Bottom: Brown/silver-colored studs; **$5–$10.**

Figure 4–18. Wrist bands, leather. Top: Purple suede/gold-colored metal; **$5–$10.** Bottom: Brown/silver-colored metal; **$5–$10.**

Figure 4–19. Hair barrettes, cloth with wood sticks. 1. Gold/white/black; **$10.** 2. Red/white/blue; **$10.** 3. Red/white/blue; **$10–$15.**

Figure 4–20. Top row: 1. Hair barrette, carved wood. 4"; **$20–$25.** 2. Cloth patch. Black/gold/blue/green; 4¾"; **$10–$15.** 3. Match book. White/black/blue/green; 2"; **$10.** Middle row: 1. Cloth patch. Red/blue/white/gold; 3"; **$8–$12.** 2. Cloth patch. White/green/black/gold; 3"; **$25.** 3. Button. Black/white; 1¾"; **$10–$15.** Bottom row: 1. Hair barrette. White/blue/red; 4"; **$5–$8.** 2. Hair barrette. Blue/red/white/gold; 3"; **$10–$15.** 3. Hair barrette. White/red/blue/yellow; 3"; **$5–$8.**

Figure 4–21. Scarf, rayon, circa 1971–72. White/blue/red; **$35–$45.**

Figure 4-22. Belt, cotton with metal loops, circa 1970. Red/white; **$25-$35.**

Figure 4-23. Belt, cotton, circa 1970-72. White/blue; **$20-$25.**

Figure 4-24. Glassware, circa 1972. Tall glass: clear with yellow, printed design; 6" tall; **$10-$15.** Mug: white milk glass with blue, printed design; $3\frac{1}{2}$" tall; **$10-$15.**

Figure 4-25. Mug, pottery, circa 1972. Japan. White/black; $3\frac{1}{4}$" tall; **$10-$15.**

Figure 4-26. Coasters, vinyl, circa 1971. Blue/white; 4" square; **$30-$35,** set of four.

Figures 4–27, 4–28, and 4–29. (three views of the same glass). Peace, Brotherhood, Freedom. Clear glass with printed design, black/blue/red/white; $5\frac{1}{2}''$ tall; **$20.**

Figure 4–30. Place mats, cotton, circa 1971–72. White/green/yellow; 15" × $10\frac{1}{2}''$; **$40–$50,** set of four.

Figure 4–32. Book End, metal with agate (stone) base, circa 1971. 6¾" tall; **$45–$50.**

Figure 4–31. Spoons, part of service for six, stainless steel, circa 1970. **$100–$150** set.

Figure 4–34. Light Bulb, circa 1968–1970. 4" tall; **$35–$50.**

Figure 4–33. Lamp, plaster, 1974. Continental Studios. Beige; 17½" tall; **$150** (rare).

Figure 4–35. Figures, peace and F.U., wood and plastic, circa 1971–73. Brown; 4"–8¾" tall; **$10–30** each.

Figure 4-36. Switchplate cover, cardboard Black/white; 6"; **$15.**

Figure 4-38. Figures, peace, wood, circa 1971-73. Brown; 6" and $6\frac{5}{16}$"; **$25-$35.**
The left-handed one is unusual.

Figure 4-37. Figure, Peace, carved wood, circa 1970-71. 25" tall (unusually large); **$125.**
Probably made in the Philippines.

Figure 4-39. Figure, plastic, circa 1971. Purple (came in other colors, also). 13"; **$25-$35.**

Figure 4–40. String Art, circa 1970–72. Black background/white nails/gold thread; 14" × 14"; $25.

String Art was a popular craft.

Figure 4–42. Poster: Things go better with peace on earth, circa 1970. Black/gold/blue/green/white; 22" × 34"; $45.

Figure 4–41. Poster, 1971. White/red/blue; 24" × 36"; $45.

Figure 4–43. Sticker, circa 1972–73. Wallfrin, Brooklin, NY. Gold/red/blue/white/black; $3\frac{3}{4}$" × $2\frac{7}{8}$"; $15.

Figure 4–44. Cloth stick-on, circa 1970–71.
*White/red/blue; $11\frac{1}{4}$" × $7\frac{1}{2}$"; **$20.***

Figure 4–45. Note Cards, 1971. Designed by Alan
Hartwell for Random Press Inc. NY, NY. White/red/
*blue; $5\frac{3}{8}$" × $4\frac{1}{4}$"; **$8–$10** each.*

Figure 4–46. Needlepoint kit, circa 1972. Purple/
*white/turquoise; 12" × 12"; **$35.***
     Would probably make a pillow.

Figure 4–47. Mobile, cardboard, circa 1971. Made
in USA. Black/white; 9" × 12", package size;
$15–$20.

Figure 4–48. Eight Track Tape Case, vinyl, circa
*1971. Black/white; $4\frac{1}{4}$" × $12\frac{1}{4}$" × $5\frac{3}{4}$"; **$40–$50.***

Figure 4–49. License Plate, circa 1971–72. White/
*blue; 6" × $11\frac{7}{8}$"; **$20.***

Figure 4–50. Dog tags, stamped aluminum. **$10–$15.**

Figure 4–51. Cinderblock, cement, circa 1971–72. $11\frac{1}{2}" \times 11\frac{1}{2}"$; **$75.**

Furniture
and
Home Decor

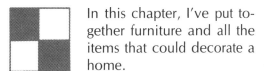
In this chapter, I've put together furniture and all the items that could decorate a home.

Interior design in the psychedelic era was very much like the clothing design. Conservative, super-mod, pop art, hippie style, psychedelic, and everything in between. And like everything else at that time, interior design went through a lot of experimentation. People tried different environments, sunken floors, indoor tents, caves, black-and-white, various hot color combinations, and smooth and glossy surfaces. They used deep-pile fake fur (and real fur) for floors, bed coverings and sometimes on walls. Some chose lots and lots of pattern; others opted for solid color.

Interior design for hippies was usually informal. It may have included floor pillows, tribal carpets and weavings (now fairly expensive, but cheap in the 1960s and 70s), old furniture which they sometimes repainted in bright enamel colors, paper flowers, live plants, posters, and whatever else interested the individuals.

Much of the so-called modern furniture of the 1960s and 1970s was actually not new at all. Designs created originally in the 1920s and 1930s were finally put into mass production 50 years later! Especially the chrome creations, like those of Bertoia, which, in the 1930s were very expensive to make. By the 1960s, new technology allowed chrome furniture to be mass produced easily. Also reproduced in chrome were the bentwood chairs originally designed by Thonet in the nineteenth century. And, made for a second time, the Knoll tables and chairs in molded fiberglass that were designed in the 1950s. (I've heard people refer to these as "the Jetson's chairs," meaning the animated cartoon!)

In the 1960s and 1970s, new inventions in inflatable plastic and molded hard plastic were utilized for furniture. These new materials gave designers the freedom to create unusual shapes, since plastic can be molded easily, while old-fashioned wood and upholstery had its limits. (See the plastic hand chair in this chapter.) The molded clear lucite "Daffodil" and "Tulip" chairs of the late 1960s were made possible by modern plastic and manufacturing technology. (There was see-through clothing, so I suppose that see-through furniture was a logical development!) The late 1960s also saw the creation of the very popular bean bag chair. A large vinyl bag filled with pellets, it was theoretically the ultimate in comfort because it molded itself to fit a person's anatomy and posture. They were also cheap and came in bright mod colors.

Like the experiments in paper clothing, there were a few creations in paper furniture—actually, a stiff cardboard. The 1960s was a "disposable" time, and the inflatable plastic and paper furniture was meant to be thrown away after it was no longer wanted.

Around 1968, the inflatable furniture, like the balloon, inspired a water-filled counterpart—the waterbed.

The butterfly chair and circle chair, a tubular metal framework with a canvas seat stretched over it, was *not* invented during the psychedelic years. I've heard dealers either call it a '50s or a '60s item. It was available in the 1964 Montgomery Ward spring catalog (for $7.95), so it definitely predates psychedelia.

Unusually shaggy carpets were popular. Pile as deep as four- or five-inches was used for "designer" rooms. (Two inches sufficed for more moderate people.) These carpets proved impractical to keep clean, however, and they had a tendency to get ratty looking with use. Op art, pop floral designs, super-graphics, and just plain bright colors were all utilized for carpeting. By the early 1970s, even linoleum came in mod styles.

Robert Indiana's famous "Love" design was used for wallpaper around 1972–73. Throughout the psychedelic period, a variety of very bright wallpapers were produced. There were experiments with metallics, mylars (shiny metallic-like, crinkly plastic), and fuzzy velours for wall coverings. Carpet was used as a wall covering, usually going part way up walls with the top part of the wall done in paint or paper. Paisley patterns, art nouveau designs from the late 1800s, early 1900s, large and small floral patterns, and op art patterns were popular. Many interior design how-to books of the early 1970s suggest using different patterned paper for different walls in a room, and papering the ceiling and floor for intense, overwhelming pattern.

Popular in the 1960s were ball-shaped chrome lamps, with the light bulb covered in a ball-shaped shade. Table lamps varied from a single fixture to a cluster of balls. Ceiling lights usually were made with three balls hanging at different heights. Floor lamps held a single large chrome ball out on a long arched stem that often was used to hurdle a couch and put the light out in front of it. A variety of mood lamps were invented in the 1960s, including the now-famous lava lamp. Rotating cylinder lights were popular in psychedelic patterns, with the rising heat from the light bulb used to spin a plastic cylinder inside a stationary cylinder. These were not a new invention, however. They were made in the 1930s and 1940s with scenes of ocean waves or a burning forest on a glass shade with a cast metal base and top.

Black lights (ultraviolet tubes or bulbs) were quite popular. Ultraviolet reactive inks were used on posters that were made for use with a black light (see the chapter on posters). Ultraviolet paint was available for body paint, too. One interior design book that I found suggested using black light to change an ordinary room for a unique party atmosphere.

Collecting Hints

Most of the things in this chapter have not been reproduced, with the exception of lamps. Lava lights, black lights, some kinds of mood lamps, and strobes are still being made. You may want to check out the new things available in the stores to get a better idea of what they look like. The new rotating plastic cylinder lamps have plastic bases and different patterns than the old ones. Lamps made around 1970 have plastic bases too, but older ones have metal bases.

Incidentally, whether you have an old or new lava lamp, *don't* use a higher wattage bulb in it than what is recommended by the maker (generally a 15 watt). A bigger bulb will ruin your lamp.

A great place to find out more on interior design in the 1960s and 1970s is your local library. Most libraries have interior decorating books from the era.

Figure 5–1. Footstool, circa 1970. Made in Taiwan. HTF. Black/white; 26" wide; $50.

Figure 5–2. Footstool, circa 1970. Vinyl covered cardboard box. Black/white; 14¼" × 14¼" × 12½"; $40–$60.

Figure 5–3. Footstool and Chair, circa 1970. Inflatable plastic. Stool: Made in Taiwan—HTF chair: Made in Taiwan, Reese Stein & Co., Inc. Black/white; Stool: 26" wide; chair: 36" wide. Stool, **$50;** chair, **$150–$250.**

Figure 5–4. Chair, circa 1970 (see color section). Molded hard plastic with plush cushion that attaches with snaps. Venture Line Furniture Co., Monroe Falls, Ohio. White with red cushion; 37" wide, 39" deep, 23" tall; **$200–$300.**

Figure 5–5. Miniature Chairs, circa 1968. Carved wood with chipmunk-fur seats (oh, gross!) Wood is painted white. Marked "HT" in a diamond on the bottom. 10½" tall.

No recent sales indicators. (A style popular in full size furniture, as well.)

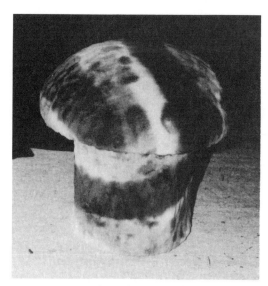

Figure 5–6. Toad Stool, plush upholstery over fiberboard and cardboard, circa 1973–74. Hassocks Inc., Columbus, MA. Brown/white/tan; 17" tall; **$50.**

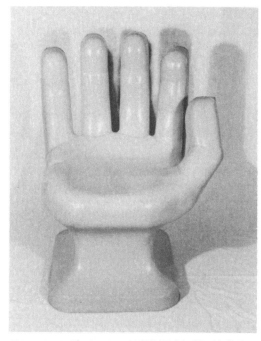

Figure 5–7. Chair, circa 1968. Molded hard plastic. Said to be made in Italy. Orange (comes in black or white, also); 35½" tall at the middle finger; **$250.**

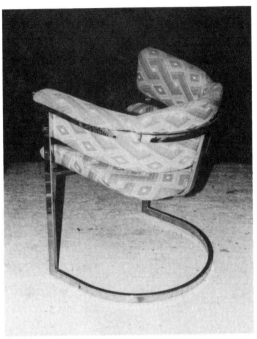

Figure 5-8. Chair, chrome and upholstered, circa 1967 (see color section). Upholstery: orange/yellow/red/olive green; 27" tall; **$250.**

Figure 5-9. Side Table, fiberboard with silkscreen print, © 1967 (see color section). By Joyce Miller, Manufactured by William Products, York, PA. Black/purple/light blue/dark blue; 16¾" tall; **$150.**

Figure 5-10. Side Table, circa 1968. Molded hard plastic. Andrew Morris for Stendig. Red; 17½" tall × 21" deep × 18" wide; **$150.**

Figure 5-11. Side Table, or if several are stacked—shelves, chrome, circa 1968-70 (see color section). 14" square, **$65** each.

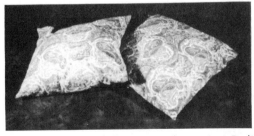

Figure 5-12. Floor Pillows (see color section). Red/white/ocher/green/blue/pink; 22" square each; **$20** each.

A popular form of hippie seating.

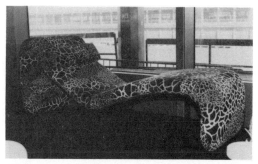

Figure 5–13. Lounge, circa 1967–68. Designed by Oliver Morg. Upholstered. Black/gold/white; 26" tall, 68" long; $1800.

Figure 5–14. Pillow, Inflatable plastic, 1970 (see color section). "Best Seal Corp., NY." Yellow/ black; 12" × 12"; $35.

Figure 5–15. Pillow, inflatable plastic, circa 1969. "Reese Stein Corp., Phila., Pa." Purple/white/ black; 12"; $10–$15.

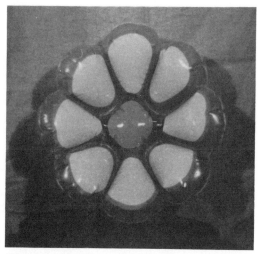

Figure 5–16. Pillow, inflatable plastic, circa 1970. "Made in Taiwan." Yellow/orange/clear plastic; 12"; $10–$15.

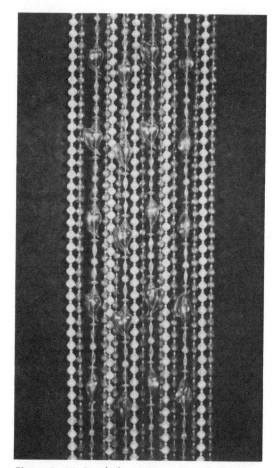

Figure 5–17. Beaded curtain section, plastic, circa 1969. Red/blue/white; 60" long strands; section 3 feet wide: $30–$60.

Figure 5-18. Curtains, cotton, circa 1970-71 (see color section). Black/white; 24" × 61" each panel; **$45-$55** a pair.

Figure 5-20. Bedspread, cotton, circa 1970-71. Black/white; **$50.**

Figure 5-19. Bedspread, cotton, circa 1968-70. (Block printed in India). Red/orange—they come in a great variety of colors and patterns; **$25-$30.**

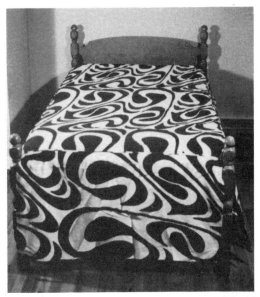

Figure 5-21. Bedspread, cotton, circa 1973. Black/white; **$50.**

65

Figure 5–22. Hanging lamp, 6-sided plastic shade, 2-bulb fixture, circa 1968–69. Blue/black; 10½" tall; $75–$150.

Figure 5–24. Lamp, rotating plastic cylinder, plastic base, circa 1970. "Synergisms, San Francisco, California." Blue/pink/green/orange/yellow; 10½" tall; $30–$35.

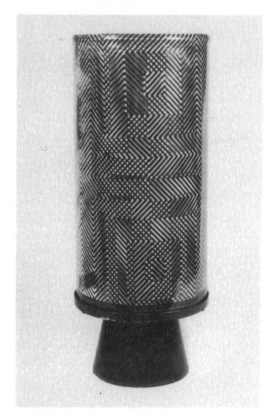

Figure 5–23. Lamp, rotating plastic cylinder, metal base, circa 1968. "Visual Effects Inc. NY. Patent Pending." Black/clear plastic/white; 14¼" tall; $45–$65.

Figure 5–25. Lamp, rotating plastic cylinder, plastic base, circa 1969–70. "Visual Effects Inc., NY." Pink/blue/black/yellow; 13¼" tall; $35–$40.

Figure 5–26. Lamp (desk or table) (see color section). Wood base and chrome; Black/chrome; 22" tall to the top of the center pole; **$50–$65.**

Figure 5–27. Lava Lamp. Red, blue, or green; 15" tall; **$50.**

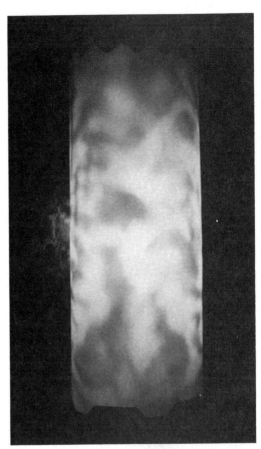

Figure 5–28. Lamp, frosted plastic cylinder, clear cylinder inside printed with a black design, with 4 small bulbs inside, circa 1970. ''The Love Light.'' 12" tall; **$20.**

Figure 5–29. Lamp, empty soda can with decal, circa 1971. Blue/white/red; $4\frac{7}{8}$" tall; **$25–$35.**

Figure 5–30. Lamp, plastic, circa 1975. "Spiderlite Mood Light, Data Display Systems Industries, Phila., Pa." Light: black/red; case: brown; $11\frac{3}{4}"$ × $11\frac{3}{4}"$ × 3"; **$45.**

Figure 5–32. Graphic Print, 1964. Artist: Victor Vasarely. Blue/red/orange/purple/brown/dark blue; 38" × 19"; **$75–$150.**

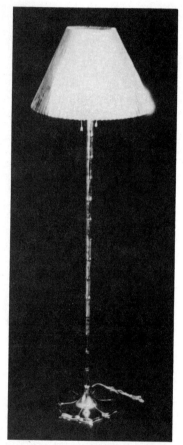

Figure 5–31. Lamp—chrome with lotus shaped base, bamboo stem. Silver-color shade (see color section). Tyndale, NY. 57" tall; **$250** a pair.

Figure 5–33. Graphic Print, circa 1972. Artist: John Alcom. White/orange/olive/brown/blue/purple/pink/yellow; 18" × 18"; **$30–$40.**

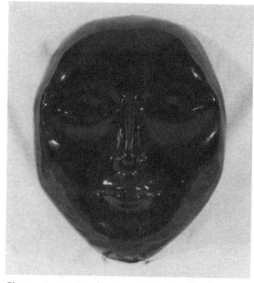

Figure 5–34. Wall decoration, molded plastic, circa 1968. Black; 16" × 20"; **$45–$75.**

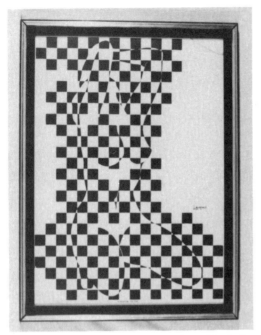

Figure 5–35. Graphic Print, circa 1968–70. Artist: Lawrence. Title: "Check Nude." White/black; 18½" × 25" (excluding the frame); **$40–$60.**

Figure 5–37. Graphic Print, circa 1968. Artist unknown. Black/white/blue/red; 12¾" × 14¾" (including the frame); **$25–$30.**

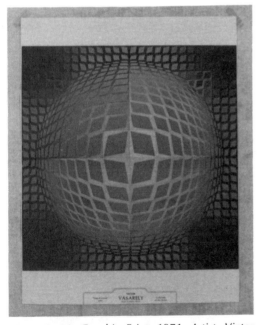

Figure 5–36. Graphic Print, 1971. Artist: Victor Vasarely. Red/blue/purple/yellow/green/black; 16¼" × 20½" (possibly cut down); **$30–$35.**

Figure 5–38. Plaque, print laminated on masonite, copyright 1970. "Fran Mar Greeting Cards Ltd." Black/white; 9" × 11"; **$15–$20.**

Figure 5–39. Area Carpet, circa 1971–72. "Textiles Manuales, Diseñadas Par Stellas, Pure Wool, Bogota, Columbia." Orange/yellow/red/brown/pink; 84" × 44"; **$100–$150.**

Figure 5–40. Clock, plastic, circa 1970. "PeaceTime, Westclox." Blue/green/white/yellow; 6½"; **$75.**

Figure 5–42. Clock, plywood face, circa 1971–72. "Sessions." Yellow/pink/green/white hands/blue butterflies; 12"; **$30–$40.**

Figure 5–41. Hangers (One of a set of four—the four seasons), cardboard, circa 1969. "Personality Hang-Ups, Framingham, Mass." Pink/brown/green/white/blue/mirrored-foil glasses; 13⅜" tall; **$60–$80** set of four.

Figure 5–43. Picture Frame, plastic, circa 1971. "Dan-Dee Import, NY, NY." Olive green/green/pink/blue/orange; 4¼" square; **$10.**

Figure 5–44. Hangers, cardboard, circa 1969. Black/white; Him: 15½" tall, her: 16" tall; **$15–$20** each.

Figure 5–45. Hanger, cardboard, circa 1969. "Manufactured Exclusively by Saunders Enterprises." Black/white; 17" tall; **$40.**

Figure 5–47. Mobile, cardboard, circa 1968–70. "Made in Japan." Flourescent: blue/red/green/orange/yellow/black; **$15–$20.**

Figure 5–48. Mobile, cardboard, circa 1970. "Mr. Mitty's Mobiles, Santa Monica, Calif." Flourescent: pink/orange/yellow/black; 16" tall; **$15–$20.**

Figure 5–46. Wall pocket letter holder, felt on board, circa 1972–74. Orange/green/white/yellow/blue/pink/purple; 8" × 24"; **$10–$15.**

Figure 5–49. Mexican "God's Eye", yarn wrapped over wood stick frame, popular 1967–74. Orange/blue/red/maroon/black/chartreuse; 19"; **$15.** Popular hippie decor.

Figure 5–51. Ice Bucket, vinyl and lucite, circa 1970. Red/orange/green/purple/white/blue; 16" tall (including the handle); **$30–$35.**

Figure 5–50. Basket, with wood balls, circa 1967. Black; 13½" at widest point; **$35–$50.**

Figure 5–52. Mobile, metal/wire/plastic balls, circa 1972 (see color section). "Made in Hong Kong." Black base, orange/yellow balls (comes in other colors also); 18½" tall; **$15–$20.**

Figure 5-53. Wig Stand, cardboard, circa 1969. Black/white; 13" tall; **$25-$35.**

Figure 5-55. Paperweight, pottery, circa 1972. White/green/yellow/orange/blue; $2\frac{1}{2}$" tall; **$15.**

Figure 5-56. Lunch Pail, metal, circa 1971-72. Blue/green/red; $9\frac{1}{2}$" (not including the handle); **$40-$60.**

Figure 5-54. Silverware Set (service for six), stainless and plastic, circa 1968. "MSC—Designer, Taiwan." Red; **$75-$100** a set.

Figure 5–57. Glass bowl (see color section). Hand blown, signed: "Molina." Blue/green; 5" wide, 3¼" tall; $30–$40.

Figure 5–58. Ash Tray, ceramic, circa 1969. Yellow/brown/pink/white/black; 7¼"; $20–$25.

Movies and Theater

6

All movies produce at least one type of collectible—a poster. But some, like Yellow Submarine, are more commercially exploited, generating many collectibles. (Probably, if Yellow Submarine hadn't been a *Beatles* movie, the manufacturers would not have been interested in making Yellow Submarine merchandise.) Although there were many interesting movies made in the psychedelic era, none has produced as much in collectible artifacts as Yellow Submarine. Therefore, there are a great number of Yellow Submarine items in this chapter. For you Beatle collectors, it is not in the nature of this book to represent *all* of the Beatles collectibles, only the *psychedelic* collectibles, such as Yellow Submarine.

Also a note: the artist who created Yellow Submarine was Heinz Edelmann, *not,* as I occasionally am told, Peter Max.

The theater has never been a source of a great variety of collectible merchandise. Their goal is to sell *tickets* to people, not stuff. And, although "Hair" was probably the most famous presentation of this period, there is little memorabilia. There is even less material from other theatrical productions. This field is basically limited to posters, programs, and articles written about the shows in the news media.

Some of the most famous poster artists produced a few theatrical posters. See Victor Moscoso's poster for "The Chairs" and Milton Glaser's poster for "The Wiz."

Collecting Hints

 If you are only interested in the Yellow Submarine collectibles, you should refer to one of the books written specifically on Beatles collectibles for more information. Beatles items have been reproduced, and some things that were made in the 1970s (post Beatles) are now collectible too!

No other movie memorabilia from this time has been reproduced.

Hair recently has been revived, but the original collectibles have not been reproduced.

Figure 6–1. Model, Yellow Submarine, 1968. Model Products Corporation. Box, 9¼" × 6½" × 3½"; toy, 9" long; $175–$250.

Figure 6–2. Toy, Yellow Submarine, 1968. Corgi Toy. Box, 6½" wide; toy, 5½" long; $325–$350.

Figure 6–3. Puzzle, Yellow Submarine, 1968. Jaymar. Box, 9½" × 8⅛"; puzzle, 18" × 13"; $65–$75.

Figure 6–4. Puzzle, Yellow Submarine, 1968. Jaymar. Box, 12¼" × 12¼"; puzzle, 19" × 19"; $75–$85.

Figure 6–5. Mobile, Yellow Submarine, 1968. Sunshine Art Studios Inc. $14\frac{1}{2}'' \times 9\frac{3}{4}''$; **$75–$100.**

Figure 6–6. Key tags, Yellow Submarine, 1968. $6\frac{1}{8}'' \times 2\frac{3}{4}''$; **$75** set of 4.

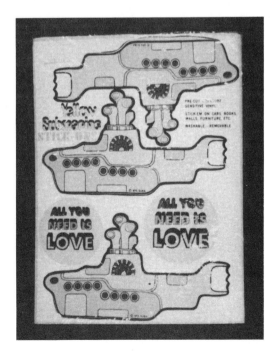

Figure 6–7. Switch plate covers, Yellow Submarine, 1968. Dal Mfg. Corp., Providence, R.I. Orange/blue/pink/red/black/yellow/purple; $6\frac{1}{4}'' \times 10\frac{1}{2}''$; **$90** set of 5.

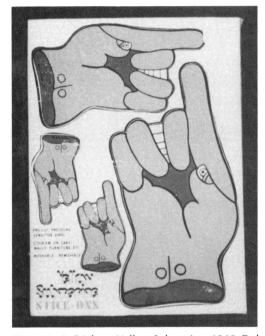

Figure 6–9. Stickers, Yellow Submarine, 1968. Dal Mfg. Corp., Providence, R.I. White/blue; $9'' \times 12''$; **$15.**

Figure 6–8. Stickers, Yellow Submarine, 1968. Dal Mfg. Corp., Providence, R.I. Yellow/orange/red/black/purple; $9'' \times 12''$; **$25.**

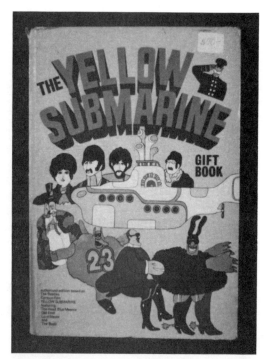

Figure 6–10. Gift book, Yellow Submarine, 1968. World Distributors Inc., Manchester, England; 8⅜" × 12"; **$70.**

Figure 6–11. Bulletin board, Yellow Submarine, 1968. KFS—Subafilms. White/black/multi-color; 7½" × 23"; **$60–$75.**

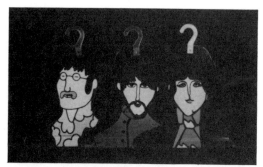

Figure 6–12. Hangers, Yellow Submarine, cardboard, 1968. King Features Syndicate, Subafilms. Henderson—Hoggard Inc. Black/multicolor; 14¾" tall; **$85** each.

Figure 6–13. Gum cards, Yellow Submarine, 1968. Anglo Confectionery Ltd. 3½" × 2½"; **$15** each card.

Figure 6–14. Book, The Beatles Yellow Submarine, 1968. Signet Books. **$20–$25.**

Figure 6–15. Post Cards, Yellow Submarine, 1968. King Features Inc., Subafilms. $10\frac{1}{4}" \times 14\frac{1}{4}"$; **$30** set of 6.

Figure 6–16. Greeting cards, Yellow Submarine, 1968. Sunshine Cards. $8\frac{3}{8}" \times 4"$; **$15** each.

Figure 6–17. Movie poster, "Fillmore," 1972. Twentieth Century Fox. David Byrd, artist. Rolled one-sheet. Multicolor; $40" \times 60"$; **$200.**

Figure 6–18. Movie poster, "Psych-Out," 1968. American International Pictures. Rolled one-sheet. White/black/multicolor; $40" \times 60"$; **$100.**

Figure 6–19. Mini poster, Hair, 1969. Tarot Productions Inc., L.A. Calif. Multicolor; $10\frac{3}{4}"$ long; **$30–$40.**

*Figure 6–20. Movie poster, ''The Trip,'' 1967. American International Pictures. Rolled One-sheet. Black/white/yellow; 40″ × 60″; **$150.***

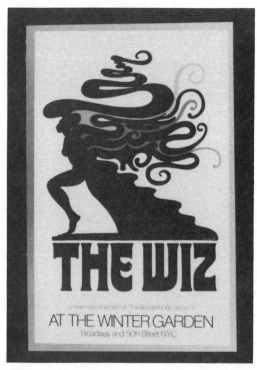

*Figure 6–21. Poster, The Wiz, 1974. At the Winter Garden, NY. Milton Glaser, artist. Black/white/green/blue/purple; 13⅞″ × 23″; **$75–$100.***

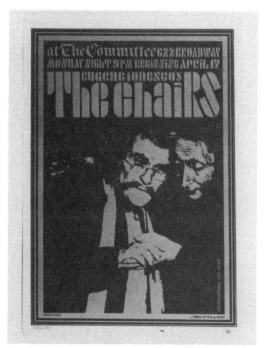

*Figure 6–22. Poster, The Chairs, April 17, 1967. The Committee Theater, San Francisco, Calif. Victor Moscoso, artist. Blue/pink/white; 15″ × 20″; **$50–$100.***

The rock show poster artists sometimes did posters for other events.

*Figure 6–23. Switchplate covers, Easy Rider, circa 1970. Cardboard. Black/white photos; 5″ × 8″; **$15** each.*

Television

The best psychedelic TV show had to be Laugh-In. It liberated TV comedy. The show dared to make jokes about sex, politics, and the world in general like nobody else had before, with a lot of mod and psychedelic graphics thrown in.

While the older generations often fumed about "kids today," and the generation gap seemed like the Grand Canyon, many older folks did enjoy Laugh-In. Because it was funny, people didn't mind the comments on politics, war, just about anything in the news, fashion, sex, or whatever the show's producers fancied. They combined political statements with vast amounts of silliness so that nobody got upset by the political statement! Characters ranged in age from little Edith Ann to the Dirty-Old-Man and Mean-Old-Lady. Laugh-In made jokes out of everything and everybody, somehow without seeming to insult anybody. Richard Nixon was a guest on the show. He said, "Sock it to Me." A variety of other celebrities that were popular with older generations, including John Wayne, appeared on the show. Laugh-In minimized the generation gap.

There is a fairly good selection of Laugh-In collectibles available. Love American Style was not quite as far out as Laugh-In, but it did produce a few collectibles.

Television tried to get the attention of the teenage population with pop music. The Monkees and later the Partridge Family filled that space and inspired a variety of toys for teen consumers which are now very collectible.

Collecting Hints

 As far as I know, no TV collectibles have been reproduced.

Figure 7–1. Toy, Laugh-In: Party, 1969. Saalfield Publishing Co., Akron, Ohio. Multi-color; 11" × 14⅜"; **$30–$35.**

Figures 7–2, 7–3. Bed spread, Laugh-In, circa 1969. Yellow/pink/blue/orange/black/green/white; **$50–$75.**

Figure 7–4. Bulletin board, Laugh-In, circa 1969. Tan/black/olive/yellow/orange; 18" × 24"; **$25.**

Figure 7–5. Greeting card, Laugh-In, 1969. 8" × 14½"; **$15.**

Figure 7–6. Clock, The Partridge Family, 1972. Time Setters, Made in USA. Multi-color photograph; 9"; **$45.**
The clock in the photograph has no hands.

Figure 7–8. Game, The Partridge Family, © 1971. Milton Bradley Company, Springfield, Mass. $9\frac{5}{8}$" × $19\frac{1}{8}$" box; **$25–$35.**

Figure 7–9. Clock, The Partridge Family, 1972. Time Setters, Made in USA. Multi-color photograph; 9"; **$45.**

Figure 7–10. Finger puppets, The Monkees, 1970. Remco Ind. Inc. 5" tall; **$100–$125,** set of three.

Figure 7–7. Model, The Monkees Monkeemobile, 1968. Corgi Toys. $6\frac{1}{4}$", box; $4\frac{7}{8}$" long, toy. **$225.**

Figure 7–11. Puzzle, The Monkees, 1967. Fairchild—The Puzzle People; © Raybert Productions Inc./Screen Gems, Inc. 13" × 10¼", box; 17" × 11", puzzle. **$35.**

There are four different puzzles in the series.

Figure 7–14. Hand puppet, The Monkees, 1965. Mattel. Yellow/orange/black/brown/pink; 9½" tall; **$75–$100—$150** if the voice works.

They have voice boxes, but they usually don't work.

Figure 7–12. Model, The Monkees Monkeemobile, 1968. Corgi Juniors. 3", toy; **$175.**

Figure 7–15. Tambourine, The Monkees, 1967. © Raybert Productions Inc./Screen Gems Inc. 8½"; **$115–$130.**

Figure 7–13. Bracelet, The Monkees, 1967. © Raybert Productions Inc./Screen Gems Inc. Gold metal with color photos; gold/white/red, card; 9", card; **$35.**

Figure 7–16. Bracelet, The Monkees, 1967. © Raybert Productions Inc./Screen Gems Inc. Gold metal; gold/white/red, card; 9", card; **$35.**

Figure 7–17. Toy guitar, The Monkees, 1966. © Raybert Productions Inc./Screen Gems Inc. Black plastic with multicolored paper print. 14" long; **$140–$160.**

Figure 7–18. Game, The Monkees, 1967. © Raybert Productions Inc./Screen Gems Inc. Transogram Co., Inc. Orange/yellow/red/pink/brown/blue/purple; 9" × 17½", box; **$115–$130.**

Figure 7–19. Thermos™, The Monkees, 1967. © Raybert Productions Inc./Screen Gems Inc. Blue with multicolored photos. 6½" tall; **$65.**

Figure 7–20. Hanger, The Monkees, Peter Tork, 1967. © Raybert Productions Inc./Screen Gems Inc. Famous Faces Inc., Norristown, Pa. Black/white; 13½" tall (not including the hanger); **$75.**

Figure 7–21. Sleepshirt, The Monkees, circa 1967. Multicolor; **$165.**

Figure 7–22. Poster, "Belle of 14th Street/Barbra Streisand," 1967. Monsanto Textiles Division Presents. CBS TV, October. Black/beige/pink/purple/brown; 21" × 29"; **$100.**

Figure 7–23. Puzzle, The Mod Squard, © 1969. Milton Bradley Company. Red/yellow/green/purple/blue/white/black/tan; $9\frac{5}{8}$" × $14\frac{1}{2}$", box; $14\frac{1}{4}$" × 20", puzzle. **$20–$25.**

Figure 7–24. Clock, Love American Style. Black/red/blue/white/green; 9"; **$125.**

Music Festivals

8

Probably the most famous three days in musical history are Woodstock in 1969. There are several highly sought after items from the actual festival: Posters, programs, buttons, tickets, and shirts. The Warner Brother's movie produced a few more collectibles.

Besides the familiar dove-and-guitar design poster, there was a poster with a stained glass window motif that was printed, but not used because the location was changed. The "original" poster by artist David Byrd may have been intended to be sold as a souvenir, since it has very little information on it about the show.

However famous Woodstock is, it was not the only music festival, nor was it the first festival of its kind. Other festivals produced some interesting collectibles, too. In particular, the poster for the Magic Mountain Music Festival in 1967 is a great one, and the poster from the Monterey Pop Festival in 1967 had a beautiful design. The disastrous Altamont Speedway show appropriately has produced no collectibles.

Collecting Hints

The Arnold Skolnick-designed dove-and-guitar Woodstock poster is being reprinted in the smaller, 18½ by 25-inch, size only. (So far, the large size poster has not been reproduced.) Unfortunately, the reprints are made from the *original printing plates* and on the same type of paper so they are difficult to detect. There were several versions of the original poster, since the names of bands were added after printing began. The reprint poster is of the last poster that listed all of the bands. The only difference I've noticed between the reprints and the originals is that the new posters are printed *exactly* on register (the colors all line up where they're supposed to be). The originals were printed more hastily, and often not in register (there are slight overlaps, or gaps between colors). Sometimes there are even ink smears. The orange color is missing completely on the poster that was photographed for this book (the ''3,'' ''of,'' and ''&'' were supposed to be orange). These posters were left over from the original printing. I'm not sure if any perfectly printed original posters exist.

No other reproductions are being made, yet.

I have been hearing about Woodstock items, particularly posters and unused tickets, having huge price tags. Although the posters are not particularly common, they are not worth thousands, either (at least not yet). There are a lot of unused tickets available. The tickets that were sold were kept by the people who were there, because nobody collected them after it became a free concert. Thousands of unsold tickets remained after the show, and were not destroyed. Tickets sell for between $35 and $50 each, not hundreds of dollars.

Figure 8–1. Poster: Woodstock, 1968 (see color section). Unused poster designed for Wallkill, NY., before the location was changed to White Lake, NY. David Byrd, artist. Multicolor. 13⅝" × 22⅜"; **$150–$250.**

Figure 8–2. Program: Woodstock. **$75–$100.**

Figure 8–3. Poster: Woodstock, 1969. Arnold Skolnick, artist. Red/white/blue/green/black/yellow/orange; 18½" × 25"; **$350;** *24" × 36";* **$450.**

Figure 8–5. Kite: Woodstock, 1970. Remco Industries Inc. Blue/pink/clear plastic; 30" × 35¾"; **$45.**

Figure 8–6. Patch: Woodstock, 1970. Blue/white/pink; 3"; **$8–$15.**

Figure 8–4. Book: Woodstock Nation, *1969, by Abbie Hoffman. Vintage Books/Random House.* **$20–$30.**

Figure 8–7. Program: Woodstock *(from the movie), 1970. Songs and Photos. Warner Brothers.* **$20–$40.**

Figure 8-8. Button: Woodstock, 1969. Blue/orange/white; $2\frac{1}{2}$"; **$25-$35.**

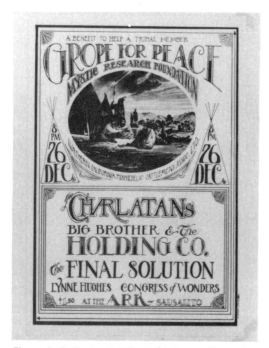

Figure 8-10. Poster: Magic Mountain Music Festival, June 3-4, 1967. Mt. Tamorats Outdoor Theatre. Miracles/The Byrds/Wilson Pickett/The Seeds/Blues Magoos/Jefferson Airplane/The Doors/Tim Harden/Sparrow/Country Joe and the Fish/Moby Grape/Mojo Men/Every Mother's Son/Loading Zone/Grass Roots/Etc. Stanley Mouse, artist. Black/silver/orange/blue; $18\frac{7}{8}$" × $27\frac{3}{4}$"; **$275-$300.**

Figure 8-9. Poster: 1st Grope for Peace, December 26, 1966. The Ark, Sausalito, CA. The Charlatans/Big Brother and the Holding Co./The Final Solution/Lynne Hughes/Congress of Wonders. Stanley Mouse, artist. White/black; $12\frac{1}{16}$" × $16\frac{15}{16}$"; Value unknown.

Figure 8-11. Poster, Hawaii Pop Rock Festival, Waikiki Shell, August 8-9, 1967. Canned Heat/Country Joe and the Fish/Luke's Pineapple Store/Blues Crew/Tony Sonoda. Victor Moscoso (Neon Rose), artist. Bright green/orange/brown; 14" × 20"; **$50.**

Figure 8−12. Poster: 2nd Annual Grope for Peace, December 26, 1967. Straight Theater, San Francisco, CA. Rick Griffin, artist. Green/red/black/white; $19\frac{3}{16}" \times 27\frac{11}{16}"$; Value unknown.

Figure 8−14. Post card: San Francisco International Pop Festival, October 26−27, 1968. Carson-Morris Studios, artist. Multicolor; $5" \times 6\frac{3}{4}"$; **$25.**

Figure 8−13. Poster: Festival of Growing Things, July 1−2, 1967. Quicksilver Messenger Service/Miller Blues Band/Blue Cheer/Sandy Bull/Hugh Maskela/Congress of Wonders/Charlatans/Ace of Cups/Wildflower/Mt. Rushmore/Big Brother and the Holding Co./Country Joe and the Fish. Also Gutt, artist. Yellow/green/white; $13\frac{7}{8}" \times 18\frac{1}{2}"$; **$150.**

Music
Concert
Posters
and
Postcards

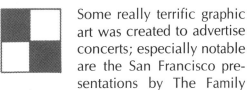 Some really terrific graphic art was created to advertise concerts; especially notable are the San Francisco presentations by The Family Dog and Bill Graham, beginning in 1966. Concert posters were made for various other San Francisco clubs, like the Matrix, the Western Front and several others, as well as many not-quite-so-famous locations all over the country. All are collectible, although the most popular are the San Francisco posters.

San Francisco could be considered the center of psychedelia. Psychedelic art, music, and light shows were first started there in 1965. Notice the names of the bands on these posters. All the popular psychedelic bands called San Francisco home. The Jefferson Airplane, the Doors, the Grateful Dead, Big Brother and the

Holding Company and a variety of less well-known psychedelic bands played at the clubs in San Francisco and other places nearby. That's not to say nothing went on anywhere else. Psychedelic art and music happened all over the country and throughout most of the world. But San Francisco was the center for it all. The largest body of high quality poster art of the psychedelic era has come out of San Francisco.

Some people collect for artistic considerations, some collect one particular favorite artist, some collect posters showing favorite bands, and some approach collecting posters like collecting stamps—they try to get a complete set.

Collecting Hints

You'll notice that there is usually a *huge* difference in the value of posters between a first printing and later printings. That makes it important for *you* to know which is which. You need either a reliable and knowledgeable dealer, an expert collector, or a copy of *A Collector's Guide to the Numbered Dance Posters Created for Bill Graham and The Family Dog: 1966–1973* by Eric King (see References in the back of this book). The differences between the printings vary from one poster to another, although a few generalities can be made. The first printings of the Family Dog from #1 to #40 have no number or credits at the bottom. (The credits on later printings are: "© The Family Dog . . ." etc.). After #41, the first printings are numbered: "No.XX–1," second printings are usually numbered "No.XX–2" and third printings are numbered "No.XX–3".

Even if you got your posters from San Francisco in the '60s, you could have reprints; because reproducing the early posters started in 1967. The concert posters were very popular. At first they were made only for advertising and not many were printed. Most of those that were hung up were quickly stolen! Then when their popularity and, therefore, commercial potential was realized, the posters were reprinted to sell. If those sold, more were printed. Beginning in 1967, posters were printed in one very large run, both for advertising and for sale.

There are "bootleg" copies of some posters made in England in the 1960s. They are marked "San Francisco Poster Company." Unless you're looking for a cheap wall-covering, don't buy them.

Some of the Fillmore posters were legally reprinted in the early 1970s, and artist Wes Wilson reprinted several posters of his in 1986 (these are dated 1986) and are collectible, although the prices are lower than the originals.

In many cases, only the later printings are available; they are a good way to get a sample of certain posters without laying out major amounts of money. After all, the *quality* of the poster wasn't changed by a later printing—only the *quantity*.

Be careful when buying early Family Dog posters. It is possible for a less-than-honest person to trim off the bottom edge to remove the number and credits and try to sell it as a first printing. The margin at the bottom should be about as wide as the margin at the top.

So far, there have been no reprints made of posters from any other club that I know of. Those were only printed once.

Posters

FAMILY DOG—THE AVALON BALLROOM.

*Figure 9–1. FD1 February 19, 1966; Jefferson Airplane/Big Brother and the Holding Co. Wes Wilson, artist. White/black; $14\frac{1}{8}$" × $20\frac{5}{8}$" reprint; 1st printing, very rare; 2nd printing, **$50.***

The first printing had no number or credits, the second printing was marked "No. 1–2" and "© Family Dog Productions, 1725 Washington Street, San Francisco" across the bottom.

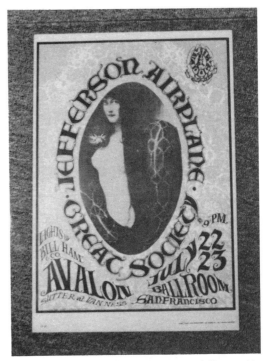

*Figure 9–2. FD17 July 22–23, 1966; Jefferson Airplane/Great Society. Stanley Mouse, artist. Purple/gold; $13\frac{15}{16}$" × $20\frac{1}{16}$"; 1st printing, **$300–$400;** 2nd printing, **$75;** 3rd printing, **$25.***

The first printing had two variations: one with gold background, the other with silver. Both are worth about the same. There are no number or credits on the first printing. The second printing adds: "17(2)" and "Bindweed Press, © Family Dog Productions 1966. 1725 Washington Street, San Francisco." The third printing changes the address to: "1966 © Family Dog Productions, 639 Gough St. San Francisco, Calif." and is numbered "17(3)."

*Figure 9–3. FD48 February 17–18, 1967. Big Brother and the Holding Co./Quicksilver Messenger Service/Oxford Circle. Stanley Mouse/Alton Kelley, artists. Brown/black/white/grey; 20" × 14"; 1st and 2nd printings, **$40–$55.***

There are two printings, both labeled "No.48–1."

Figure 9–4. FD17A July 15–16, 1966 (this concert was cancelled). Love/Big Brother and the Holding Co. Stanley Mouse, artist. White/purple, other colors weren't printed, 14″ × 20″; Only one printing, $500.

This poster is very rare. The show was cancelled when the poster was in production, so it was not finished. Only 500 posters were printed.

Figure 9–5. FD22 August 19–20, 1966. Grateful Dead/Sopwith Camel. Alton Kelley/Stanley Mouse, artists. Yellow/black/white; 14¼″ × 20½″; 1st and 2nd printing, $200–$300; 3rd printing, $30–$40.

The 1st and 2nd printings are identical: Both have no number and are credited to "The Bindweed Press, San Francisco." The third printing has: "© Family Dog Productions, 1725 Washington Street, San Francisco."

Figure 9–6. FD32 October 28–29, 1966. The Quicksilver Messenger Service/Blackburn & Snow/ Sons of Champlin. Victor Moscoso, artist. Purple/ black/white; 14 3/16″ × 19 7/8″; 1st and 2nd printing, $300–$500.

The first and second printings are exactly the same. No number.

Figure 9–7. FD35 November 18–19, 1966. Daily Flash/Quicksilver Messenger Service/Country Joe and the Fish. Stanley Mouse, artist. Blue/red/white/black; $13\frac{3}{4}$" × $19\frac{15}{16}$"; 1st and 2nd printing, **$150;** 3rd printing, **$30–$40.**

The first and second printings are the same. They have no number, and credit "The Bindweed Press, San Francisco". The third printing is numbered "No.35–3" and has "© Family Dog Productions, 1725 Washington Street, San Francisco." An unauthorized copy was also made by the San Francisco Poster Co. in England.

Figure 9–8. FD41 December 30–31, 1966. Country Joe and the Fish/Moby Grape/Lee Michaels. Stanley Mouse/Alton Kelley, artists. Orange/blue/black/white/red; 14" × $20\frac{1}{2}$"; 1st printing, **$75;** 2nd printing, **$30.**

The first printing is numbered "41–1." The second is numbered "41–2."

Figure 9–9. FD45 January 27–28, 1967. Grateful Dead/Quicksilver Messenger Service. Stanley Mouse/Alton Kelley, artists. Light brown/green/red/white; 14" × $20\frac{1}{4}$"; only 1 printing, **$100.**

This poster was printed once, numbered "No. 45–1."

*Figure 9–10. FD47 February 10–11, 1967. Miller Blues Band/Lee Michaels/Peanut Butter Conspiracy. Victor Moscoso, artist. Orange/blue/pink; $14\frac{1}{16}$" × $19\frac{7}{8}$"; 1st printing, **$50**; 2nd printing, **$30**.*

The first and second printing are both numbered "No.47–1," but the first printing has the color listed above, the second has green instead of the blue.

*Figure 9–11. FD49 February 24–25, 1967. Moby Grape/The Charlatans. Victor Moscoso, artist. Orange/blue/bright pink; 14" × 20"; 1st, 2nd, and 3rd printings, **$35–$55**.*

Three printings, identical, numbered "No.49–1."

*Figure 9–12. FD69 July 4, 1967. Quicksilver Messenger Service/Siegal Schwall/The Phoenix. Rick Griffin, artist. White/black/brown; $14\frac{1}{2}$" × $21\frac{3}{4}$"; 1 printing, **$50–$60**.*

Figure 9–13. FD59 April 28–29, 1967. Chamber's Brothers/Iron Butterfly. Victor Moscoso, artist. Blue/pink/orange; 14" × 20"; 1st and 2nd printing, **$30–$40.**

There are two printings, both numbered "No.59–1."

Figure 9–15. FD64 June 1–4, 1967. Miller Blues Band/Doors/Daily Flash. Victor Moscoso, artist. Blue/pink/green; 13⅞" × 19¹⁵⁄₁₆"; 1st and 2nd printings, **$50–$65.**

This poster was printed twice, identical, numbered "No.64–1."

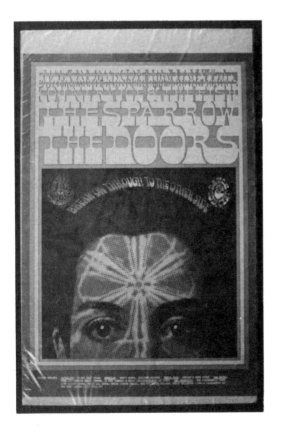

Figure 9–14. FD50 March 3–4, 1967. The Doors/ The Sparrow/Country Joe and the Fish. Victor Moscoso, artist. Green/red/blue; 13¹⁵⁄₁₆" × 20"; 1st, 2nd, and 3rd printings, **$50–$60.**

There are three printings, all numbered "No.50–1."

Figure 9−16. FD70 July 6−9, 1967. Siegal Schwall/ Miller Blues Band. Victor Moscoso, artist, Eric Weber, photographer. Pink/blue/black/yellow/orange/green; 14″ × 20$\frac{1}{16}$″; 1st and 2nd printings, $30−$45.

Poster was printed twice, identical, numbered "No.70−1."

Figure 9−17. FD74 August 3−6, 1967. Charles Lloyd Quartet/West Coast Natural Gas Co./Tripping West to East. Bob Fried, artist. Red/purple/pink/ blue/silver (or white); 14″ × 20″, 1st printing, $50; 2nd printing, $30.

Only the first printing has the silver. Both are numbered "No.74−1."

Figure 9–18. FD62 May 19–21, 1967. Quicksilver Messenger Service/Country Joe and the Fish. Rick Griffin, artist. White/green/yellow/orange/blue/ black; 19$\frac{15}{16}$" × 14"; 1st printing, $35–$45.

Only printed once.

Figure 9–19. FD76 August 17–20, 1967. Quicksilver Messenger Service/The Other Half/Melvyn Q. Jack Hatfield, artist. Metallic silver/blue/red/ white; 13$\frac{15}{16}$" × 20"; $35–$45.

This poster was printed only once.

Figure 9–20. FD–D6 October 13–14, 1967. Van Morrison/Daily Flash. Stanley Mouse/Alton Kelley, artists. White/black/red/orange; 14$\frac{1}{8}$" × 20"; $35–$45.

This poster was printed only once.

Figure 9–21. FD95 and FD–D13 December 1–2 & 8–10, 1967. Jim Kweskin/Sons of Champlin & Jim Kweskin/Solid Muldoon. Victor Moscoso/Rick Griffin, artists. Purple/blue/orange/pink/white/yellow/green; 14" × 20", each poster; $50 each, $100 pair.

Both posters were printed only once.

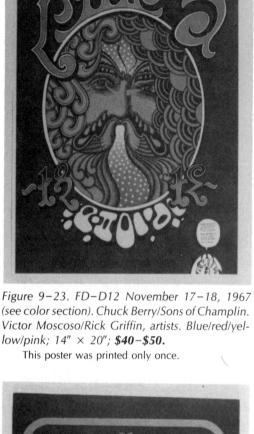

Figure 9–23. FD–D12 November 17–18, 1967 (see color section). Chuck Berry/Sons of Champlin. Victor Moscoso/Rick Griffin, artists. Blue/red/yellow/pink; 14" × 20"; $40–$50.

This poster was printed only once.

Figure 9–22. FD96 December 15–17, 1967. Quicksilver Messenger Service/The Charlatans/ Congress of Wonders. Stanley Mouse/Alton Kelley, artists. Lavender/blue/pink/black; 11¼" × 20½"; $30–$50.

This poster was printed only once.

Figure 9–24. FD100 January 5–7, 1968. Youngbloods/Ace of Cups. Charles Laurens Heald, artist. Black/pink/green/blue/yellow; 14" × 20"; $30–$50.

This poster was printed only once.

Figure 9−25. FD102 January 19−21, 1968. Genesis/Siegal Schwall/Mother Earth. Bob Fried, artist. Black/blue/yellow/red; 14″ × 20″; $30−$50.
This poster was printed only once.

Figure 9−27. FD119 May 17−19, 1968. Junior Wells/Sons of Champlin/Santana Blues Band. Bill Henry, artist. Blue/pink/gold/brown/white; $13\frac{7}{8}$″ × $19\frac{7}{8}$″; $30−$50.
This poster was printed only once.

Figure 9−26. FD117 May 3−5, 1968. Junior Wells/ Canned Heat/Crome Syrcus/Clover; Carl Lundgren, artist. Black/gray/pink/orange/yellow/blue/ green; $13\frac{5}{8}$″ × 20″; $30−$50.
This poster was printed only once.

Figure 9–28. FD120 May 24–26, 1968. Young-bloods/Kaleidoscope/Hour Glass. John Thompson, artist. Blue/orange/yellow/green/brown/white; 13⅝" × 20"; $30–$50.

This poster was printed only once.

NOT IN THE NUMBERED SERIES, EVENTS AT THE AVALON BALLROOM

Figure 9–29. A Zenefit; November 13, 1966. (Benefit for Zen Mountain Center.) Grateful Dead/ Big Brother and The Holding Co./Quicksilver Messenger Service. Robert Bono, photographer. Black/ lavender; 12⁷⁄₁₆" × 19⅞"; $75–$100.

Figure 9–30. Krishna Consciousness Comes West; January 29, 1967. Swami Bhaktivedanta/Allen Ginsberg/Grateful Dead/Moby Grape/Big Brother and the Holding Co. Unknown artist. Pink/purple/red; 12⅞" × 19¾"; $50–$75.

BILL GRAHAM—THE FILLMORE AUDITORIUM

Figure 9–31. BG1 February 4–6, 1966. Jefferson Airplane. Peter Bailey, artist. Yellow/red; 14¼" × 19 15/16" 1st printing, $400–$500; 2nd printing, $100–$200; 3rd printing, $50.

The first printing was done on yellow index paper, which is yellow on both the front and back. "Design Peter Bailey, East Wind Printers" appears faintly near the bottom with type running up the edge. The second printing has no credit to the designer and printer; otherwise it is the same as the first. The third printing is on white index which is *printed* with yellow on the front only and credited to "Creative Lithograph Co. No. 1."

Figure 9–32. BG24 August 19–20, 1966. Young Rascals/Quicksilver Messenger Service. Wes Wilson, artist. White/green/orange; 13¾" × 20½"; 1st printing, $75–$100; 2nd/3rd printing, $50–$65.

The first printing has union logo #221 in the lower right. The other two printings do not.

Figure 9–34. BG33 October 23, 1966. Yardbirds/ Country Joe and the Fish. John H. Myers, artist. Purple/black/white; 14" × 20"; 1st printing, $100–$150; 2nd/3rd printing, $35–$50.

The first printing had union logo #221 in the lower right corner. The other two printings had no union logo and added "Printing by West Coast Lithograph Co., S.F."

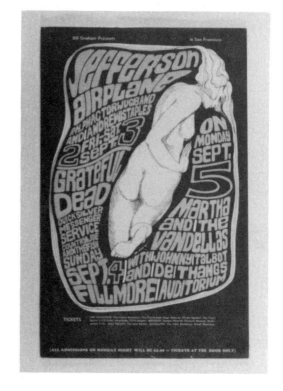

Figure 9–33. BG26 September 2–5, 1966. Jefferson Airplane/P.H. Phactor/Andrew Staples/Grateful Dead/Quicksilver Messenger Service/Country Joe and the Fish/Martha and the Vandellas/Johnny Talbot and De Thangs. Wes Wilson, artist. Black/ pink/white; 13⅜" × 20⅞"; 1st printing, $250–$300; 2nd printing, $65–$75.

The first printing has no number "26." The 2nd printing adds (faintly) a "26" after Wes Wilson's signature.

Figure 9–35. BG34 October 28–30, 1966. Captain Beefhart and his Magic Band/Chocolate Watch Band/The Great Pumpkin. Wes Wilson, artist. Red/ blue/light blue/pink/white; 1st printing, $150; 2nd printing, $45–$55.

The difference in the two printings is the size. Allowing for a slight variation, the first printing measures $13\frac{5}{8}$" × $19\frac{1}{8}$", the second printing $13\frac{11}{16}$" × 19".

Figure 9–36. BG38 November 18–19, 1966. Grateful Dead/James Cotton Blues Band/Lothar and the Hand People. Wes Wilson, artist. Red/ orange/gray/dark blue; $13\frac{1}{2}$" × $20\frac{3}{8}$" (this is a 1986 reprint); 1st printing, $125–$150; 2nd printing, $75. Reprinted by Wes Wilson, 1986, $15–$20.

The first printing has a darker gray background and measures $13\frac{1}{2}$" by about $21\frac{3}{16}$" long, the second printing has a lighter gray background, and measures about 21" long. The Wes Wilson 1986 reprint is glossy, and has "Copyright © 1986 Wes Wilson" in the lower left.

*Figure 9–37. BG42 December 16–18, 1966. Jefferson Airplane/Junior Wells/Chicago Blues Band/Tim Rose. Wes Wilson, artist. Aqua blue/purple/orange-red; 1st printing, 14" × 22¼"; 2nd printing, 14" × 22¹³⁄₁₆". 1st printing, **$50–$60;** 2nd printing, **$40.***

*Figure 9–38. BG45 January 13–14, 1967. Grateful Dead/Junior Wells/Chicago Blues Band/The Doors. Wes Wilson, artist. Green/purple/red/black; 14" × 22"; **$50–$65.***

There are two printings, but they are very similar.

*Figure 9–39. BG54 March 10–12, 1967. Jefferson Airplane/Jimmy Reed/John Lee Hooker/Stu Gardner Trio. Wes Wilson, artist. Orange/purple/lavender/pale green; 13³⁄₁₆" × 20⁷⁄₁₆"; **$50–$60.***

This poster was printed only once.

Figure 9–40. BG53 March 3–5, 1967. Otis Rush and his Chicago Blues Band/The Mothers/The Morning Glory. Wes Wilson, artist. Black/white/blue/pink/green/yellow/red; 1st printing, $13\frac{7}{16}"$ × $22\frac{1}{2}"$; 2nd printing, $13\frac{1}{2}"$ × $22\frac{7}{16}"$. 1st printing, **$75–$85;** 2nd printing, **$50–$60.**

    The color and size differ between the two printings. The first printing is blue/green at the top of the square of lettering, while the second printing is a pale yellow there.

Figure 9–41. BG59 April 14–16, 1967. Country Joe and the Fish/Loading Zone. Peter Bailey, artist. White/purple/ocher/pink; $13\frac{5}{16}"$ × $21\frac{3}{4}"$; **$50.**
    This poster was printed only once.

*Figure 9–42. BG60 April 21–23, 1967. Howling Wolf/Big Brother and the Holding Co./The Harbinger Complex. Wes Wilson, artist. Blue/red/orange/maroon/yellow; 14" × 22¾"; **$50–$80.***

This poster was printed only once.

*Figure 9–43. BG64 May 19–20, 1967. Martha and the Vandellas/The Paupers. Bonnie MacLean, artist. Chartreuse/blue/red; 14" × 23"; **$40.***

This poster was printed only once.

Figure 9–44. BG73 July 18–23, 1967. Sam & Dave/ James Cotton Blues Band/Country Joe and the Fish/ Loading Zone. Bonnie MacLean, artist. Pink/dark blue/yellow; 14" × 21"; $50–$65.

This poster was printed only once.

Figure 9–46. BG67 June 9–10, 1967. The Doors/ Jim Kweskin Jug Band. Bonnie MacLean, artist. Ocher/pink/black; 14" × 23"; $85–$100.

This poster was printed only once.

Figure 9–45. BG82 September 7–9, 1967. The Byrds/Loading Zone/LDM Spiritual Band. Jim Blashfield, artist. Green/orange/purple; 14\frac{1}{8}" × 21"; $45–$55.

This poster was printed only once.

Figure 9–47. BG97 December 14–16, 1967. Tim Buckley/Chambers Brothers/Mothers of Invention. Stanley Mouse, artist. Blue-gray/white/black/red/green/yellow; $12\frac{3}{4}$" × $21\frac{7}{8}$"; **$100–$125.**

This poster was printed only once.

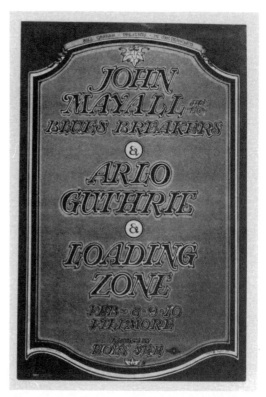

Figure 9–49. BG106 February 8–10, 1968. John Mayall and the Blues Breakers/Arlo Guthrie/Loading Zone. Stanley Mouse, artist. Red/green/black/yellow; 14" × $21\frac{1}{2}$"; **$300–$400.**

This poster was printed only once.

Figure 9–48. BG105 February 1–4, 1968 (see color section). Jimi Hendrix/John Mayall/Albert King. Rick Griffin, artist. Red/white/black/olive/blue/yellow/orange; $13\frac{7}{8}$" × $21\frac{7}{8}$"; Original printing, **$800;** reprint, **$125.**

The reprint is on glossy paper; the original has a matte finish.

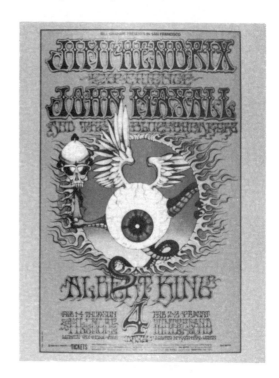

Figure 9–50. BG110 March 7–10, 1968. The Cream/James Cotton Blues Band/Jeremy & the Satyrs/ Blood, Sweat, and Tears. Stanley Mouse, artist. Yellow background/black (made from red & green printed over each other); $13\frac{15}{16}$" × $21\frac{1}{16}$"; Original printing, **$500;** reprint, **$75–$100.**

    The reprint is on glossy paper; the original on uncoated, dull paper.

Figure 9–52. BG87 October 5–7, 1967. Quicksilver Messenger Service/Grass Roots/Mad River. Bonnie MacLean, artist. Light blue/yellow/purple; 14" × $21\frac{1}{16}$"; Original printing, **$45–$55;** reprint, **$25–$30.**

    The reprint is on glossy paper; the original is dull.

Figure 9–51. BG133 August 13–25, 1968. The Who/James Cotton/Magic Sam/Creedence Clearwater Revival/It's a Beautiful Day/Albert Collins/ Grateful Dead/Kaleidoscope/Albert Collins/ Quicksilver Messenger Service/Spooky Tooth/Cold Blood. Rick Griffin and Alton Kelley, artists. Black/ red-orange/yellow/pink/purple/blue/green/white; $28\frac{3}{8}$" × 22"; **$150–$200.**

    This poster was printed only once. (Notice the large size.)

Figure 9–53. BG119 May 9–11, 1968. Loading Zone/Chrome Syrcus/H.P. Lovecraft/Tiny Tim. Weisser, artist. Black/yellow/orange/white/pink; 14" × 21"; $60–$70.

This poster was printed only once.

Figure 9–55. BG113 March 28–30, 1968. Country Joe and the Fish/Steppenwolf/Flamin' Groovies. Dana W. Johnson, artist. Black/yellow/white/blue-red-yellow dot screen; 13⅞" × 21⅞"; $85–$100.

This poster was printed only once.

Figure 9–54. BG209 December 31, 1969. Santana/It's a Beautiful Day/Elvin Bishop Group/Joy of Cooking/Jefferson Airplane/Quicksilver Messenger Service/The Sons/Hot Tuna. Bonnie MacLean Graham, artist. Black/white/blue/pink/purple/yellow/green; 27¾" × 20¾"; $125–$150.

This poster was printed only once.

Figure 9–56. BG245 July 28–August 9, 1970. Ten Years After/Cactus/Toe Fat/It's a Beautiful Day/Elvin Bishop/Boz Scaggs/Procul Harum/Leon Russell/Blodwyn Pig/Fleetwood Mac/Buddy Miles/Albert Collins. David Singer, artist. Black/blue/red/white; 28" × 21¼"; $250–$400.

This poster was printed only once.

Figure 9–57. BG136 September 12–14, 1968. Big Brother and the Holding Co./Santana/Chicago Transit Authority. Rick Griffin, artist. Blue/red/yellow/black/orange/pink; 14" × 22"; $85–$100.

This poster was printed only once.

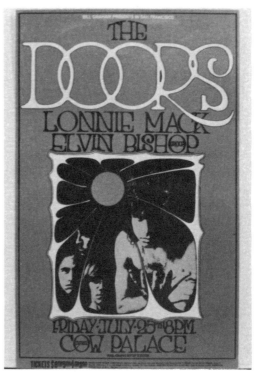

Figure 9–59. BG186 July 25, 1969. The Doors/Lonnie Mack/Elvin Bishop. Randy Tuten, artist. Red/white/black. Original printing, 13 15/16" × 21 7/8"; reprint, 14" × 21 3/4". Original printing, $125–$150; reprint, $50.

The reprint has a "W" after "records" in the ticket outlet section.

Figure 9–58. BG250 September 24–27, October 1–4, 1970. Chuck Berry/Buddy Miles/Loading Zone/Eric Burdon and War/Seals and Crofts/Clover. David Singer, artist. White/black/orange/brown/green/yellow; 28" × 22"; $150.

This poster was printed only once. It is a double size.

Figure 9–60. BG257–258 November 19–29, 1970. Love with Arthur Lee/James Gang/Black Sabbath/Sha Na Na/Elvin Bishop/Tower of Power. Norman Orr, artist. Red/dark brown/yellow/white/pink/orange; 28 1/8" × 21 5/16"; $125.

This poster was printed only once. It is a double size.

Figure 9–63. BG273–274 March 11–21, 1971. Poco/Siegal Schwall/Wishbone Ash/Sons of Champlin/Mark Almond/Commander Cody. Norman Orr, artist. Black/red/orange/yellow/white; 28" × 21⅞"; **$125.**

This poster was printed only once.

Figure 9–61. BG247 August 24–September 6, 1970. Iron Butterfly/Aum/Black Oak Arkansas/John Mayall/Elvin Bishop/Herbie Hancock/Savoy Brown/Fairport Convention/Chicken Shack/Johnny Winter/Boz Scaggs/Freddie King. Alton Kelley, artist. Black/white/red/yellow/pink; 22" × 28³⁄₁₆"; **$125.**

This poster was printed only once.

Figure 9–62. BG270 February 11–21, 1971. Fleetwood Mac/Tom Rush/Clover/Steppenwolf/Cold Blood/Shiva's Head Band/Buddy Guy/Junior Wells/It's a Beautiful Day/Blues Image/Tower of Power. Pierre, artist. White/black/red/yellow; 28³⁄₁₆" × 21³⁄₁₆"; **$300.**

This poster was printed only once.

Figure 9–64. BG263 December 31, 1970. Cold Blood/Elvin Bishop/Boz Scaggs/Voices of East Harlem/Grateful Dead/New Riders of the Purple Sage/Stoneground. David Singer, artist. Red/blue/black/gold/grays/tans; 21" × 28"; **$125.**

This poster was printed only once.

Figure 9–65. BG275 March 25–28 and April 1–4, 1971. Eric Burdon and War/J. Geiles Band/War/ Santana/Buddy Miles/Wayne Cochran/C.C. Riders/ Sugarloaf. David Singer, artist. White/red/blue/ black; $21\frac{1}{16}$" × 28"; **$150.**

This poster was printed only once.

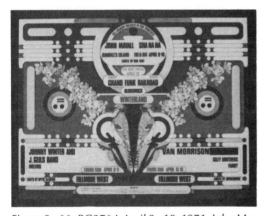

Figure 9–66. BG276A April 8–18, 1971. John Mayall/Sha Na Na/Grand Funk Railroad/Bloodrock/ Johnny Winter and J. Geiles Band/Dreams/Van Morrison/Isley Brothers/Fanny. Willyum Rowe, artist. Pink/pale yellow/purple/blue/green/black/ brown/white; $28\frac{1}{16}$" × $21\frac{1}{4}$"; **$150.**

This poster was printed only once.

Figure 9–67. BG279 & 280 May 6–16, 1971 (two posters). Miles Davis/Elvin Bishop Group/Mandrill/ Humble Pie/Swamp Dogg/Shanti. David Singer, artist. Orange/black/white; 14" × 21" each; **$50** each.

Both posters were printed only once.

Figure 9–68. Poster. Not in the numbered series event at the Fillmore and Matrix. Popcorn Happening, April 22 & 29, 1966. Singing Mothers LSD Relief Society Studio, artist. White/black; $13\frac{13}{16}$" × 20"; **$35–$45.**

117

Figure 9–69. BG287 June 30–July 4, 1971 (the last concert). Fillmore West—Closing Week. Boz Scaggs/Cold Blood/Stoneground/It's a Beautiful Day/Elvin Bishop/Grootna-Lamb/Grateful Dead/ New Riders of the Purple Sage/Rowan Brothers/ Quicksilver Messenger Service/Hot Tuna/Yogi Phlegm/Santana/Creedence Clearwater Revival/ Tower of Power/San Francisco Musician's Jam. David Singer, artist. Sky-blue/black/white; 27⅞" × 21⅞"; $300–$500.

This poster was printed only once. It is the last of the numbered series and is double size.

THE FILLMORE EAST—NEW YORK

Figure 9–70. BGE#3 April 12–13, 1968. Butterfield Blues Band/Charles Lloyd Quartet/Tom Rush. Jon Stahl, artist. Black/blue/white/pink/ orange/yellow/red/brown/ greens; 14⅛" × 21¹⁵⁄₁₆"; $50–$60.

Figure 9–71. BGE#4 April 19–20, 1968. Mothers of Invention/James Cotton Blues Band. Hersh, artist. Blue/red/white/brownish-purple; 14⅛" × 22¹⁄₁₆"; $50–$60.

Figure 9–72. BGE#5 April 26–27, 1968. Traffic/ Blue Cheer/Iron Butterfly. Fantasy Unlimited, artist. Pink/orange/white/black; $30–$60.

Figure 9–73. BGE#6 May 3–4, 1968. Jefferson Airplane/The Crazy World of Arthur Brown. Fantasy Unlimited, artist. Pale yellow/brown/green/ orange/black; 13" × 22¼"; $50–$60.

Figure 9–74. BGE#9 May 24, 1969. Ravi Shankar. David Byrd, artist. Blue/green/black; 14" × 22"; $30–$60.

Figure 9–75. BGE#11 May 20–June 27, 1971. The Final Concerts. David Byrd, artist. Yellow/turquoise/orange/black; 18" × 25$\frac{9}{16}$"; $50–$75.

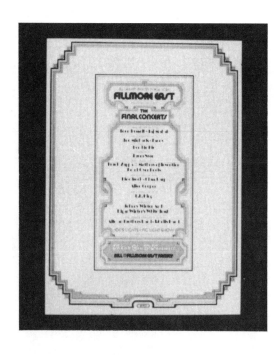

OTHER BILL GRAHAM CONCERTS

Figure 9–76. Cow Palace, San Francisco, November 20, 1973. The Who. David Singer, artist. Black/white; 18$\frac{7}{8}$" × 25$\frac{1}{2}$"; $150.

Figure 9–77. Honolulu International Center, January 21–22, 1973. The Rolling Stones. David Singer and Satty, artists. (Satty was the artist for Figure 10–15). Gray/red/blue/black/yellow/green/white; 20$\frac{3}{16}$" × 28$\frac{1}{2}$"; $200–$300.

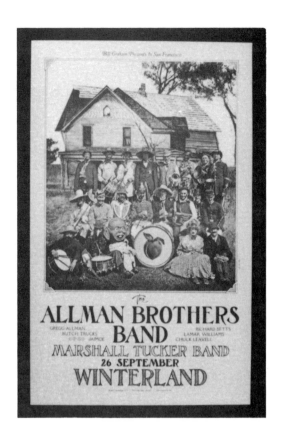

Figure 9–78. Winterland, September 26, 1973. Allman Brothers Band/Marshall Tucker Band. David Singer, artist. Dark brown/yellow/white; $13\frac{13}{16}$" × $22\frac{1}{16}$"; $35–$45.

THE MATRIX, SAN FRANCISCO

Figure 9–79. Matrix, November 22–27, 1966. James Cotton and his Chicago Blues Band/The Wildflower. Carol Behan: Fish Prods., artist. Black/white; $14\frac{3}{8}$" × $19\frac{15}{16}$"; $45.

Figure 9–82. Matrix (Neon Rose), January 31– February 5, 1967. Big Brother and the Holding Co. Victor Moscoso, artist. Green/bright pink/orange; 14" × 21"; $50.

Figure 9–80. Matrix, December 20–23, 1966. Steve Miller Blues Band/Congress of Wonders. Victor Moscoso, artist. Black/red; 14⅛" × 20⅞"; $150.

After doing three posters for the Family Dog, Moscoso produced a poster for the Matrix and negotiated with them to produce the Neon Rose series.

Figure 9–81. Matrix (Neon Rose), January 17–22, 1967. Big Brother and the Holding Co. Victor Moscoso, artist. Blue/bright pink/orange; 13¹³⁄₁₆" × 20"; $45–$55.

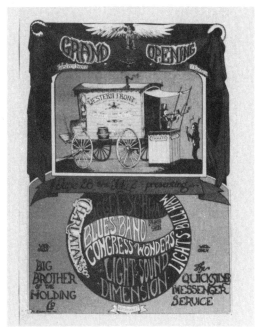

Figure 9–83. Western Front #2, June 28–July 2, 1967 (Grand Opening). The Charlatans/Siegal-Schwall/Congress of Wonders/Big Brother and the Holding Co./Quicksilver Messenger Service. Greg Irons, artist. Blue/red/black/white/pink/dark purple; 14" × 20"; **$40–$60.**

Figure 9–85. Western Front, October 13–14, 1967. Morning Glory/Indian Head Band. John Thompson, artist. Purple/orange/white; $13\frac{15}{16}$" × $22\frac{9}{16}$"; **$65.**

Figure 9–84. Western Front #3, July 7–8, 1967. Sandy Bull/Congress of Wonders/Light Sound Dimension/The Hobbits. Greg Irons, artist. White/black; $14\frac{1}{4}$" × $20\frac{1}{4}$"; **$40.**

*Figure 9–86. Western Front, December 1–3, 1967. Young Bloods/Wildflower/Initial Shock. Hovel, artist. Brown/white/red/green; 15$\frac{7}{8}$" × 22$\frac{15}{16}$"; **$65.***

THE CONTINENTAL BALLROOM

*Figure 9–87. Continental Ballroom, August 4–5, 1967. James Cotton Blues Band/Quicksilver Messenger Service/Congress of Wonders/the Ace of Cups. Grass Hopper, artist. Orange/purple/blue/white; 13$\frac{7}{8}$" × 19$\frac{5}{8}$"; **$45.***

124

PAULEY BALLROOM

Figure 9–88. Pauley Ballroom, June 25, 1967. Country Joe and the Fish/The New Age. Tom Weller—Joyful Wisdom Ent., artist. Brown/orange/blue; $14\frac{1}{4}$" × $22\frac{1}{4}$"; **$65.**

FINNISH BROTHERHOOD HALL, SAN FRANCISCO

Figure 9–89. Finnish Brotherhood Hall, January 6–14, 1966. Country Joe and the Fish/the Wildflower/John Fahey. L.S. Rehbock, artist. Red/white/orange; 14" × 20"; **$50.**

THE CAROUSEL BALLROOM,
SAN FRANCISCO

*Figure 9–90. Carousel Ballroom, April 12–13,
1968. Moby Grape/It's a Beautiful Day/Sweet
Rush. Blue/orange-red/white; $8\frac{1}{2}$" × $14\frac{1}{2}$"; $40.*

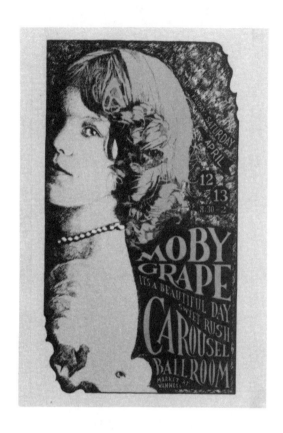

UNIVERSITY OF SAN FRANCISCO

*Figure 9–91. U.S.F., April 14, circa 1967. The
Turtles/The Freudian Slips. Patrick Ford—Progres-
sive Litho., artist. Green/orange/white; $13\frac{15}{16}$" ×
20"; $75.*

Figure 9–92. U.S.F., April 15, circa 1967. Quicksilver Messenger Service. (Though it looks like BG24, by Wes Wilson, I do not think it's his work.) Black/blue/white; 13$\frac{15}{16}$" × 20"; **$75.**

BERKELEY COMMUNITY THEATRE

Figure 9–93. Berkeley Community Theater, August 25–26, 1967. Dave Van Ronk/Mimi Farina/Fred Neil. Greg Irons, artist. Red/maroon/black/white/purple; 14" × 19$\frac{15}{16}$"; **$85.**

Figure 9–94. Berkeley Community Theatre, March 30, 1967. Jimmy Reed/John Lee Hooker/Chas. Lloyd/Miller Blues Band. Stanley Mouse, artist. White/black; 13$\frac{9}{16}$" × 18$\frac{7}{16}$"; **$75.**

CALIFORNIA HALL, SAN FRANCISCO

Figure 9–95. California Hall, July 28–30, 1967. Big Brother and the Holding Co./The Charlatans. Greg Irons, artist. Green/chartreuse/white/black; 13$\frac{15}{16}$" × 20$\frac{3}{8}$"; **$60.**

Figure 9–96. California Hall, April 16, 1966. The Charlatans/Wanda and her Birds/Slaxon—the slight of Head Magician/The Mystery Trend/The Haight St. Jazz Band. Michael Ferguson (a member of the Charlatans), artist. White/black; $13\frac{7}{8}"$ × $19\frac{15}{16}"$; $300.

OTHER CONCERTS

Figure 9–97. California Hall, April 23, 1967. Charles Lloyd Quartet/Big Brother and the Holding Co./Wildflower. Michael Wood/Pyxis Studios, artist. Yellow/black/red; 14" × 20"; $65.

Figure 9–98. Oakland Stadium, October 9–10, 1976. The Who/the Grateful Dead. Philip Garris, artist. Green-brown/amber/brown/green/black; $20\frac{1}{4}"$ × $28\frac{1}{2}"$ (this is a reprint). I don't know exact size of original poster. Original, $85; unauthorized reprint, $5.

Reprints are on glossy paper.

Figure 9–99. Honolulu International Center, July 25–27, 1969. Grateful Dead/It's a Beautiful Day. Rick Griffin, artist. Red/black/blue/purple/yellow/green; 12⅛" × 19⅞"; (this is the unauthorized new copy; I don't know exact size of large original poster.) Original large poster, **$2,000;** original small poster, **$25** (reprinted later); unauthorized new copy, **$5.**

Before this concert was cancelled, a few large posters were made. After it was cancelled, Rick Griffin had the poster reprinted in a smaller size for sale. Recently it has been copied again. The new copies are on very thin glossy paper.

Figure 9–100. Candlestick Park, San Francisco, August 29, 1966. The Beatles/the Cyrkle/the Ronettes/the Remains. Wes Wilson, artist. White/black/red/purple/yellow; 17¼" × 24"; 1st printing, **$1500;** 2nd printing, **$600.**

The outlines of the center rectangle are yellow in the first printing. No yellow appears on the 2nd printing.

Figure 9–101. Arizona State University Stadium, March 20, 1976. "A Star is Born" Live Performance. Barbra Streisand/Kris Kristofferson/Peter Frampton/Santana/Montrose/Graham Central Station/L.A. Jets. Black/orange/pink/metallic silver/metallic gold/blue/green/tan/brown/white border; 27" × 41"; **$125.**

This was to be filmed for the concert scenes in the movie.

Figure 9–102. Rolling Stones Tour, 1969. David Byrd, artist. Orange/white/blue/tan/purple/red/green/yellow; 14" × 21⅝"; **$20.**

There are a lot of these around.

THE EAST COAST

Figure 9–103. University of Michigan, Union Ballroom, November 22, 1968. SRC/Up/Brat/Carnal Kitchen. Shamie/Grimshaw, artist. Purple/blue/green/orange/red/white; 12¼" × 9½"; **$50.**

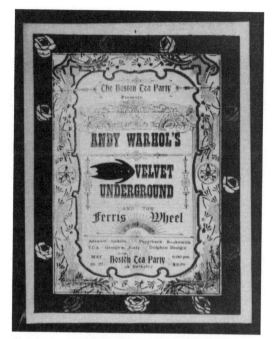

Figure 9–104. Boston Tea Party, May 26–27, 1967. Andy Warhol's Velvet Underground/Ferris Wheel. D. Arthur Haha, artist. White/green/red/blue/black/yellow; 8½" × 11"; **$100.**

Figure 9–105. Cafe Au Go-Go, New York, April 28, 1967. Dave Van Ronk/The Mothers/Ian and Sylvia. Gail Cochran—Liberty Graphics Inc., artist. Pink/blue/green/pale blue/orange/white; 7" × 10"; **$35.**

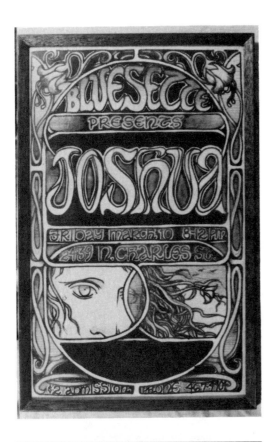

Figure 9–106. Bluesette, Baltimore, Maryland, March 10, 1967. Joshua. Barbara Smiley, artist. White/black (this particular poster is additionally hand-colored); 10¾" × 17"; $40.

Figure 9–107. Anderson Theatre, New York City, circa 1968. Hells Angels present The Grateful Dead. Blue/white/black/maroon/red/yellow; 22⅞" × 34¾"; $750.

Only 100 posters of this size were printed. But it was produced in a smaller size, also.

Figure 9–108. Tree Frog, Baltimore, Maryland, December 31, 1970. James Cotton Blues Band/Sea Train/Joshua/Glory Road/Grin. White/black; 32" × 17⅝"; **$65.**

Postcards

Figure 9–109. Double Postcard (two postcards, printed together and not separated). BG68 & 69 June 16–17 & June 20–25, 1967. The Who/Loading Zone/Jefferson Airplane/Gabor Szabo/Jimi Hendrix. Bonnie MacLean and Clifford Charles Seeley, artists. Orange/purple; 9⅛" × 7⅛"; **$40–$60.**

Double cards are scarce. They are printed on the back with: BG68: postcard back, and BG69: Fillmore summer series. They are possibly worth more than I estimate them.

Figure 9–111. Double postcard (two postcards printed together and not separated). BG99 & 100 December 26–31 & December 31, 1967. The Doors/Chuck Berry/Big Brother and the Holding Co./Quicksilver Messenger Service/Jefferson Airplane. Bonnie MacLean, artist (both). Blue/black/orange/pink/chartreuse/white/green/yellow; 9 5/16" × 7"; **$40–$60.**

Nothing printed on the back of either one. Possibly worth more than listed.

Figure 9–110. Double Postcard (two postcards, printed together and not separated). BG90 & 89 October 26–28 & October 19–21, 1967. Pink Floyd/Lee Michaels/Clear Light/Eric Burdon and the Animals/Mother Earth/Hour Glass. Bonnie MacLean (both), artist. Black/red/pink/gold/yellow/orange; 4½" × 14"; **$70–$85.**

The postcard BG90 has nothing on back.

Miscellaneous Posters

For centuries, posters have been a way of making public announcements. In the nineteenth century, slave auctions, presidential candidates, and traveling medicine shows were advertised through posters stuck up in public places. In the 1960s, posters advertised rock concerts, presidential candidates, and protests. But also, they became a form of inexpensive art to be hung indoors. They didn't necessarily advertise anything. Sometimes, posters expressed an opinion about politics or a favorite musical personality. But often, they were simply decorative art. The period 1967 to 1969 especially produced some beautiful decorative posters. Later, in the '70s, they seemed to degenerate into those flocked-background black light posters, which were not as well designed.

Peter Max posters are discussed in chapter 11. They are good examples of art that everyone could afford.

I have included in this chapter a few posters by Robert Indiana, a pop artist. He is the creator of the famous Love design that was seen everywhere about 1972. He neglected to copyright his design, so it has been used freely by everyone.

Psychedelic designs also can be found on other advertising posters from this time. Anything that someone wanted to sell to younger people was illustrated in a psychedelic style. Travel, movies, and a variety of merchandise were touted with psychedelic designs. Teens dressed in mod clothing were used to attract young consumers to manufacturer's products. The designs 7-up soda used in the Peter Max's style are worth noting. (Some people claim Peter Max did design them, others say definitely not. I found an ad in a Life magazine that had the artist's name on it—and it was not Peter Max.)

Collecting Hints

Presently, the major collecting emphasis seems to be on music posters, and Peter Max posters. So *other* posters could be a good buy as long as they have a nice graphic style.

There are no reprints of most of the posters in this chapter. The Richard Avedon posters of the Beatles, however, are being reproduced with all four Beatles printed on the same poster with ''The Beatles'' printed across the middle.

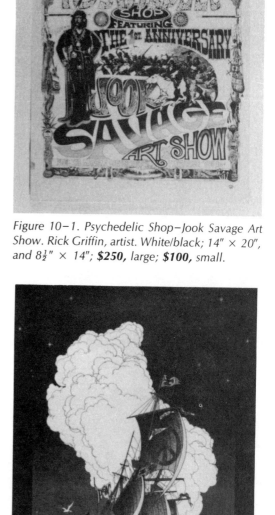

Figure 10–1. Psychedelic Shop–Jook Savage Art Show. Rick Griffin, artist. White/black; 14" × 20", and 8½" × 14"; $250, large; $100, small.

Figure 10–2. Black Light poster, © 1970. Bunnell, artist. Black/blue/white/orange/pink/purple/yellow; 24" × 38"; $35.

Figure 10–3. San Francisco Job Co-op, © 1967. Astro Posters, Berkeley, Calif. #6. John Thompson, artist. Red/yellow/purple/white; 19″ × 25″; **$100–$150.**

Figure 10–5. "Mr. Experience", © 1967 (see color section). Pandora Productions. Myers/Johansen III, artist. Blue/fuschia/red/yyellow/black, silkscreen on blue paper; 23″ × 35″; **$150–$200.**

Figure 10–6. Sunday Ramparts. Stanley Mouse/ Alton Kelley, artists. Red/brown/blue/black/white; $20\frac{1}{8}$″ × $13\frac{1}{8}$″; **$65–$85.**

Figure 10–4. Dylan. Milton Glazer, artist. Black/ white/brown/pink/orange/blue/green; $21\frac{7}{8}$″ × $32\frac{15}{16}$″; **$100.**

Figure 10–7. "Man", © 1967. Astro Posters, Berkeley, Calif. #5. John Thompson, artist. Blue/red/purple/white; 19" × 25"; **$65–$75.**

Figure 10–9. The Santa Fe Opera 20th Season, 1976. Robert Indiana, artist. Orange/blue/dark blue/metallic silver; 22" × 31"; **$200–$250.**

Figure 10–8. New York City Center Anniversary, 1968 (see color section). Robert Indiana, artist. List Art Poster 1968, HKL Ltd., printer. Blue/red/orange/metallic silver/green; 25" × 35"; **$200–$250.**

Figure 10–10. Paul McCartney. Pro-Arts, Kent, Ohio. Blue/orange/yellow, silk screen; 32" × 42"; **$75–$100.**

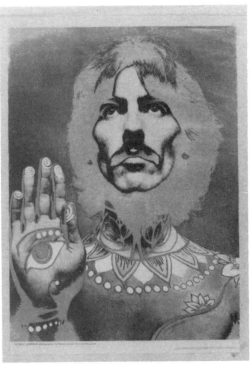

Figure 10–11. George Harrison, 1967 (see color section). Look Magazine. Richard Avedon, artist. Green/orange/white; 22⅜″ × 31″; **$75.**

Figure 10–13. Paul McCartney, 1967 (see color section). Look Magazine. Richard Avedon, artist. Light blue/green/pink/white; 22⅜″ × 31″; **$75.**

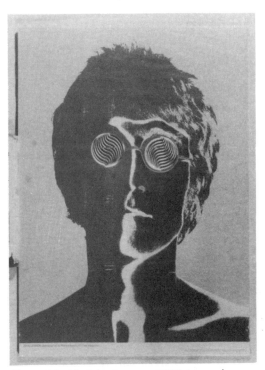

Figure 10–12. John Lennon, 1967 (see color section). Look Magazine. Richard Avedon, artist. Yellow/red/purple/white/green; 22⅜″ × 31″; **$75.**

Figure 10–14. Ringo Starr, 1967 (see color section). Look Magazine. Richard Avedon, artist. Brown/blue/white; 22⅜″ × 31″; **$75.**

Figure 10–15. "Turn On Your Mind", © 1967 (see color section). East Totem West, Mill Valley, CA, printed by Orbit Graphic Arts. Satty, artist. Pink/turquoise/white/purple; 23" × 35"; **$50–$100.**

Figure 10–16. Jimi Hendrix Memorial, © 1970. Hip Products, Chicago, IL. Edward Phelps Jr., artist. Purple/blue/black/orange black light poster; $22\frac{5}{16}$" × 30"; **$35–$45.**

Figure 10–17. Family Dog Productions, San Francisco, CA. Paul Kegan, photographer, Berkeley. Purple/orange/yellow; 24" × $22\frac{5}{8}$"; **$100.**

 Posters produced by the Family Dog, of Avalon Ballroom fame. See Chapter 9, Music: Concert Posters.

Figure 10–18. "Flight Patterns", © 1967. East Totem West, Mill Valley, CA. J.W. McHugh, artist. Red/pink/blue/green/white; 23" × 35"; **$45.**

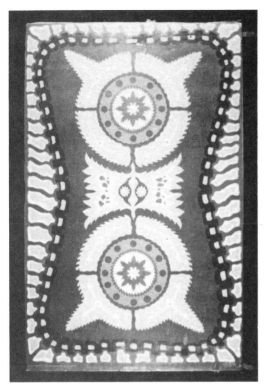

Figure 10–19. "Aquarian Age" circa 1967. East Totem West, Mill Valley, CA. J.W. McHugh, artist. Purple/yellow/green/pink/orange/black/blue; $21\frac{7}{8}$" × 34"; **$45.**

Figure 10–21. Black light poster, circa 1970. "Peace." Platt Manufacturing Co., Los Angeles, CA. T.W. Korpalski, artist. Black/orange/pink/blue/yellow/green; 24" × 35"; **$35–$40.**

Figure 10–20. Black light poster (velvet), © 1972. "Lunar Dragons." Velva-Print/AA Sales Inc., Seattle, WA. Leon Hendrix E-S-C, artist. Black/orange/blue/red/green/yellow; $34\frac{7}{8}$" × 23"; **$10–$15.**

Late "velvet" posters generally are not worth much.

Figure 10–22. "Magical Mystery Tour", © 1967. Astro Posters, Berkeley, CA #10. Eli Leon, artist. Purple/yellow/green/blue/pink/orange, black light poster; $22\frac{3}{16}$" × $34\frac{3}{4}$"; **$45.**

If you were trying to figure it out, it says: "Happy New Age" in the design.

Figure 10−23. "Masked Bath", © 1968. East Totem West, Mill Valley, CA. Nick Nickolds, artist. Purple/pink/yellow/turquoise/green/white; 22" × 33½"; $45.

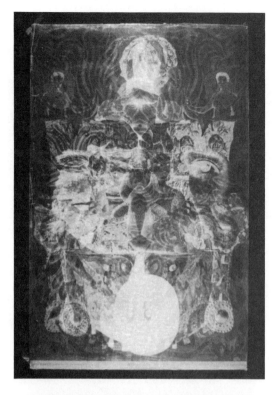

Figure 10−24. Black light poster, circa 1970−71. Insight Unlimited, Chicago, IL. Black/yellow/blue/green/pink; 15⅝" × 27⅛"; $20.

140

Figure 10–25. Black light poster, © 1969. "Garden of Eden." Hip Products Inc., Chicago, IL. Bunnell, artist. Red/blue/black/orange/yellow/green/purple/white; 22" × 35"; $25–$35.

Figure 10–26. Black light poster, © 1970. "Desert Blossom." Star City, Hollywood, CA/Specific Screen, Santa Monica, CA. Red/pink/blue/turquoise/green/yellow/purple; 26" × 40"; $35.

Figure 10−27. Black light poster, © 1970. "El Condor." Star City Distributing Inc., Los Angeles, CA. Black/white/blue/purple/pink/orange; 40" × 26"; **$35.**

Figure 10−29. Led Zeppelin—Houses of the Holy (advertising the album). White/red/orange/pink/yellow/black/green/blue; $24\frac{1}{8}$" × $35\frac{1}{2}$"; **$25.**

Figure 10−28. Black light poster, circa 1970. Black/blue/pink/green/orange/purple/yellow; $17\frac{1}{4}$" × $27\frac{1}{4}$", including the frame; **$20-$25.**

Figure 10−30. Ecology, 1971. Green/white/light green; 22" × 34"; **$35.**

Figure 10−31. The Print Mint, San Francisco, CA. Opening, December 1, 1966. Maroon/pink/white; $15\frac{1}{2}$" × $20\frac{3}{8}$"; **$125.**

Peter Max

Peter Max must be the most prolific artist of all time. From 1967 to the present he has painted, created limited edition prints, and designed a *vast* amount of mass-produced merchandise. I have a selection of the mass-produced merchandise from 1967 to 1974 in this chapter.

Peter Max has put his designs on every possible printable surface. You could cover yourself from head to foot in his designs, including shoes, tights, pants, shirts, jackets, scarves, ties, jewelry, belts, and sunglasses. Even the thin metal frames of sunglasses didn't escape his attention. For the home he designed a selection of sheets, pillowcases, towels, bedspreads, curtains, shower curtains, inflatable furniture, pillows, glassware and dishes, ashtrays, napkins, clocks, and graphic posters. He also created a variety of luggage and carrying bags, cards and stationery to send to friends, an umbrella with which to keep dry, Peter Max cereal to eat from a Peter Max bowl, gift wrap for special occasions, and bus billboards to admire on the way to work.

Peter Max wanted to make everyone's lives more beautiful. Until he came along, ordinary things were pretty boring and drab. Consider that, at one time, sheets and pillowcases were all white, towels were plain pastels, dishes and curtains commonly were in plain monotones, or with little flowers on them, and sneakers were just plain sneakers. Peter Max put *art* on ordinary things. Now those ordinary things are collectible art!

Collecting Hints

 Although his creations were originally made to sell fairly cheaply, Peter Max items are now collectible merchandise and can be very expensive. Sotheby's sold 34 posters for $33,000. (That's not original paintings, that's mass-printed posters.) I was unable to find out exactly which posters were sold.

Of the thousands of "production" posters that were released, how many actually remain in circulation? They are certainly not easy to find. There isn't any Peter Max item you can say is particularly common, although I think some of the books are relatively easier to find.

No reproductions or reprints have been made. Peter Max owns the copyrights to all of his designs, and is not interested in reproducing anything. He continues to work on *new* ideas.

There are no original posters in a $11\frac{1}{4}"$ × 16" size—these are pages taken out of the Poster books. Don't buy them!

All designs in this chapter copyright © Peter Max.

Figure 11–1. 1. Poster Book, © 1970. Crown Publishers, NY. 2. Superposter Book, © 1971. Crown Publishers, NY; **$65–$85** each.

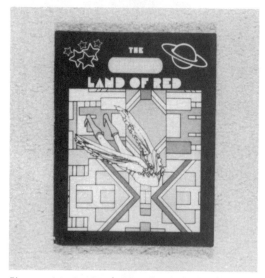

Figure 11–2. Book, Land of Red, © 1970 (hardcover). Franklin Watts Inc., NY. **$30–$50.** (There is also Land of Yellow, and Land of Blue.)

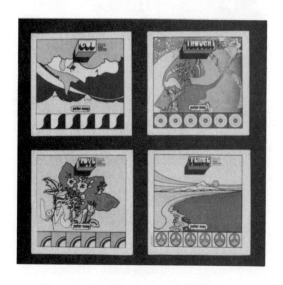

Figure 11–3. Books, God, Thought, Love, and Peace, © 1970. William Morrow and Company, Inc., NY. $5\frac{3}{4}"$ × $5\frac{3}{4}"$; **$25–$30** each.

Figure 11-4. Book, Meditations, © 1972. Mc-Graw-Hill Book Company. $6\frac{1}{4}" \times 6\frac{3}{4}"$; **$35-$45.**

Figure 11-5. Book, The Peter Max Book of Needlepoint, © 1972, by Peter Max and Susan Sommers Winer. Pyramid Books. $5\frac{1}{2}" \times 8\frac{1}{2}"$; **$30-$50.**

Figure 11-6. Book, Teen Cuisine, © 1969. By Abby Gail Kirsch and Sandra Bangilsdorf Klein. Parent's Magazine Press, NY. $6\frac{1}{4}" \times 9\frac{1}{4}"$; **$50-$75.**

Figure 11-7. Book, The Ambassador's Ball. **$100-$150.**

Recovered ''Peace'' book, made to commemorate the 24th anniversary of Israel event in Maryland, on June 19, 1972. The guest was the ambassador of Israel.

Figure 11–8. Book, Paper Airplane Book, © *1971. Pyramid Books.* $4\frac{1}{4}" \times 7"$; ***$25–$35.***

Figure 11–10. Magazine, Peter Max Magazine, No. 1, © *1970. (There are no other issues.) Peter Max Enterprises.* $12" \times 9"$; ***$35–$45.***

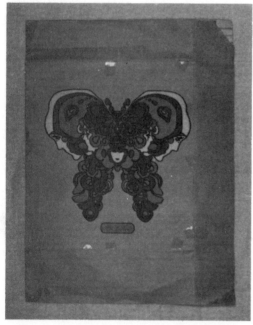

Figure 11–9. Book cover, paper, circa 1969–70. Orange background, multi-color design; $21" \times 14"$ *(photo shows $\frac{1}{2}$ of the cover);* ***$20–$25,** unused.*

Figure 11–11. Poster, "Flapper," No. 5 (no date, circa 1967). © *Peter Max Poster Corp. Yellow/blue/ pink/orange/white/green/brown;* $24" \times 36"$; ***$300.***

Figure 11–12. Poster, "Keystone Cops," No. 7 (no date, circa 1967). © Peter Max Poster Corp. Yellow/pink/red/blue/green/orange; 24" × 36"; **$300.**

Figure 11–14. Yellow pages, Manhattan, 1970. Pink/red/multi-color; 9" × 11" × 3¼"; **$50.**

Figure 11–15. Poster, "Siblings," No. 10 (no date, circa 1967). © Peter Max Poster Corp. Browns/orange/white/green/red/blue; 24" × 36"; **$350.**

Figure 11–13. Poster, "Cleopatra," No. 8 (no date, circa 1967). © Peter Max Poster Corp. Pink/greens/blue/oranges/yellow; 24" × 36"; **$300.**

Figure 11–16. Poster, "Jazzmobile," No. 13 (no date, circa 1967). © Peter Max Poster Corp., NYC. White; Circular design: rainbow-color; People: black/white; Beer bottle: brown; 24" × 36"; **$350–$400.**

Figure 11–17. Poster, "Top Cat," No. 19, 1967. © Peter Max Poster Corp., NY. Black/white; Flourescent: blue/green/yellow/pink; 24" × 36"; **$250.**

Figure 11–18. Poster, "Love," No. D, 1968. © Peter Max Poster Corp., NYC. Shades of: blue/pink/green/orange/purple/white; Overprinted lettering in purple; 24" × 36"; **$500;** Without the gallery overprinting: **$300.**

This is the standard "Love" poster, overprinted to advertise an exhibit of Peter Max's paintings at the William Zierler Gallery in New York City. The original painting for "Love" was in the exhibit.

Figure 11–19. Poster, "Dove," No. 20, 1968 (see color section). © Peter Max Poster Corp., NY. Blue/ pink/orange/yellow/green/lavender; 24" × 36; $300.

Figure 11–20. Poster, "Moon Landing," No. 1, 1969. © Peter Max Poster Corp., NYC. Shades of: purple/pink/blue/yellow/green/orange; 24" × 36"; $250.

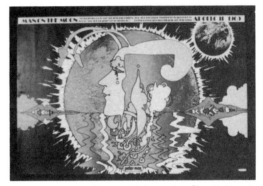

Figure 11–21. Poster, "Moon Landing," No. 3, 1969. © Peter Max Poster Corp., NYC. Black/purple/greens/pinks/blues/yellow/white/ gray/etc.; 24" × 36"; $250.

Figure 11–22. Poster, "Paint Your Wagon." © Peter Max Poster Corp., NY. Gray/brown/black/ white and multi-color; 24" × 36"; $250.

Figure 11−23. Poster, "Paint Your Wagon." ©
Peter Max Poster Corp., NY. Silver/multi-color; 24"
× 36"; **$250.**

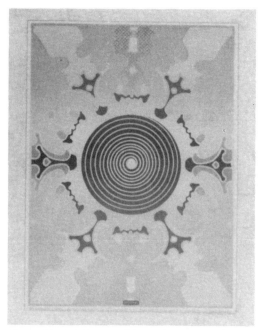

Figure 11−25. Poster, "The Visionaries at the East
Hampton Gallery on 22 West 56th Street, N.Y.C.
from March 21 to April 8. Bruno Palmer-Poroner
Director." Pink/yellow/green/blue/white; 18" ×
$24\frac{1}{8}$"; Rare, no recent sale information.

Figure 11−24. Poster, Kinney Shoes (see the color
section). Advertising for the Peter Max Sneakers.
24" × 36"; No recent sale information.

Figure 11-26. Poster, "Cloud Walking Shoes by Peter Max", circa 1971. Laconia Shoe Company, Inc., Laconia, New Hampshire; Various shades of: blue/pink/orange/purple/green/yellow/white/black/gray (pastel tones); 24" × 36"; No recent sale information.

Figure 11-27. Poster, "Our Gang." No. C, 1967. © Peter Max Poster Corp. Blue/purple/yellow/pink/green; 24" × 36"; **$250-$300.**

This particular poster is autographed, so it is worth more.

Figure 11-28. Greeting Card Sales Album, © 1974. Regency Card Co. Vinyl ringbinder filled with samples of cards, prices, ordering information, etc. (Book): orange/pink/white; **$400-$600.**

Figure 11-29. Greeting Card, © 1974 (photo taken from the card album.) Regency Card Co. (Unused): **$15.**

Figure 11–30. Puzzle, © 1970. Life, *Schisgall Enterprises Inc.*, NY. Multi-color; Box: 8½″ × 11″, puzzle: 13″ × 20″; **$40–$50.**

Figure 11–31. Puzzle, © 1970. Life, *Schisgall Enterprises Inc.*, NY. Multi-color; Box: 5⅜″ × 7⅜″, puzzle: 6¾″ × 11″; **$35.**

Figure 11–32. Chair, Inflatable Lounge, © 1971. (The bottom section folds under the seat to make a chair.) White/orange/yellow/blue/red/black/green; 55″ long; **$300–$400.**

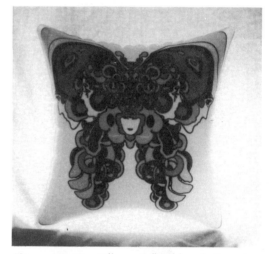

Figure 11–33. Pillow, inflatable plastic, circa 1969–70. Made in Japan. White/yellow/blue/orange/green; 15½″ × 16″; **$30.**
   There are eight different pillow designs.

Figure 11–34. Pillow, made from a needlepoint kit, circa 1972. Black/orange/blue/red/white/purple/green/yellow; 16½″ × 19″; **$65.**

*Figure 11–35. Pillowcase, circa 1970. Mohawk. Black/lavender/orange/yellow/pink/white background; 30" × 20"; **$65–$75** a pair.*

*Figure 11–36. Bed Sheet, circa 1970. Mohawk. Orange/pink/yellow/blue/maroon/black/white background; 66" × 94"; **$125.***

(The photo shows the top ⅓ of the sheet—the rest is plain white.)

*Figure 11–37. Curtains, circa 1971 (see color section). Orange/blue/yellow/white/green/pink (all pastel shades). 25" × 42" each panel; **$85** a pair.*

*Figure 11–38. Wall Clock, 1968. General Electric. (With original magazine ad, 1968, showing all six designs.) Clock: black/green/blue/orange/pink/yellow/fluorescent red hands/yellow second hand; 9"; **$85–$125.***

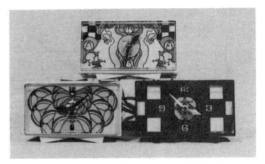

*Figure 11–39. Alarm Clocks, circa 1968. General Electric. Top: Case: white; Face: multi; left: Case: yellow; Face: multi; Right: Case: black; Face: multi; 3¼" tall, 5½" wide; **$65–$85** each.*

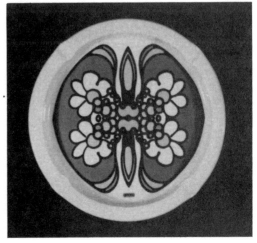

*Figure 11–40. Ashtray, pottery, circa 1968. Iroquois China, Syracuse, NY. White/brown/black/orange/pink/blue/green; 10"; **$40–$60.***

Figure 11-41. Serving Tray, metal, circa 1970. Blue/red/yellow/pink/green/lavender; 13"; **$35.**

Figure 11-43. Towel, circa 1970. Tastemaker by Mohawk. Blue/white stars/red saturns/orange Peter Max logo; 25" × 42"; **$40-$50.**

Figure 11-42. Plate, glass, circa 1967. Houze Glass Co. White/blue/red/yellow/pink/black; $9\frac{3}{8}$"; **$40-$50.**

Figure 11-44. Plate, glass, circa 1967. Houze Glass Co. White/purple/yellow/green/orange-pink; 7"; **$30-$40.**

Figure 11–45. Serving tray, fry-pan, and coffeepot. Enamel on metal, circa 1973. Ernest Sohn Creations, Japan. Tray, red with orange/white/purple/ blue; 13½"; **$35.** Fry-pan, green outside; yellow/ red/blue/black inside; blue edge; 13" long, including the handle; **$75–$100.** Coffeepot, green with red/yellow/gray/green design outside; yellow inside; blue edge and knob; 8½" tall; **$100–$200.**

Figure 11–46. Borden Yogurt tub, vinyl, circa 1969–70. Pink/black/white/red/yellow/green/ blue; 10½" tall; No recent sale information.

Seems to be a rare item. I haven't seen any others yet, and people I've talked to didn't know it existed.

Figure 11–47. Box, Love—Swiss Mixed Cereal box, 1970 (see color section). © Peter Max Enterprises. Manufacturer: Somalon AG. Sachseln, Switzerland; US Importer: Richter Brothers Inc., NY, NY. Yellow/pink/orange/red/green/blue/black/ white; Box; 5" × 7¼" × 1½"; No recent sale information.

This item is inherently perishable, so I imagine there are very few left.

Figure 11–48. Cup, Jello Pudding, plastic, 1972, (for making Jello instant pudding). © Peter Max Enterprises Inc. Yellow/red/black; 7⅜" tall; **$35.**

*Figure 11–49. Necklace, circa 1968. Ceramic pendant, vinyl thong; Blue/green/orange/pink/white; 3⅜"; **$40–$60.***

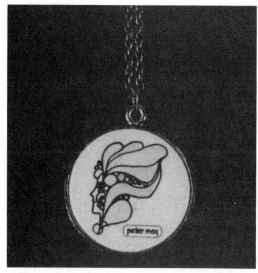

*Figure 11–51. Necklace, circa 1969. Enamel on silver-color metal. Made in Western Germany. Yellow/pale green/pale orange/black; 2⅜"; **$35–$50.***

*Figure 11–50. Necklace, circa 1968. Ceramic pendant, vinyl thong. Green/red/orange/yellow/blue/black/white ceramic; 3⅜"; **$40–$60.***

*Figure 11–52. Pins, circa 1969. Enamel on silver-color metal. Made in Western Germany. 1. Yellow/red/orange/green/lavender; 3". 2. Pale blues/green/yellow/orange/lavender, 2½". 3. Green/white/yellow/black; 2⅝"; **$40** each.*

*Figure 11–53. Belts, circa 1970. Designed by Peter Max Enterprises for Canterbury. Cloth with metal buckles. Top: White/yellow/red/black/silver buckle. Bottom: Red cloth with Buckle: yellow/blue/white/red/pink buckle silver frame; **$50** each.*

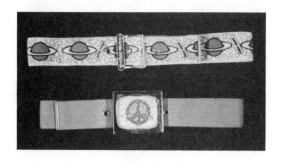

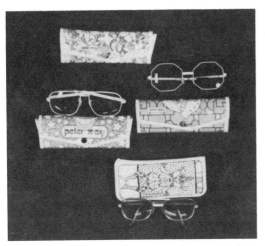

Figure 11-54. Sunglasses and cases, circa 1969-70. **$100** a pair of glasses and a case. (The glasses are also Peter Max designs, with his logo on them.)

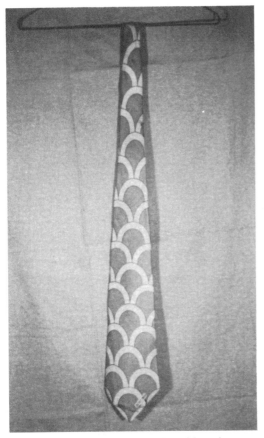

Figure 11-55. Tie. Orange/yellow/blue; **$50.**

Figure 11-56. Sneakers, circa 1968 (see color section). Randys. **$300-$400;** (With the original box in the color section: **$500.**)

Figure 11-57. Shirt, 1974. Expo '74—Preserve the Environment. T-Shirt Gallery, NY Red shirt, printed with blue/green/white/red/yellow/purple/pink; **$50-$75.**

Figure 11-58. Button, 1972. Green/blue/brown/white; $1\frac{1}{2}$"; **$75-$100.**

Figure 11–59. Jacket, circa 1969. Mr. Wrangler (wool). Blue/red/gold/gray; lining: purple/white; **$300–$450.**

Figure 11–61. Umbrella, vinyl, circa 1968–69. Made in USA. Yellow/purple/green/gray/black/white; $26\frac{1}{2}$" tall; **$300–$500.**

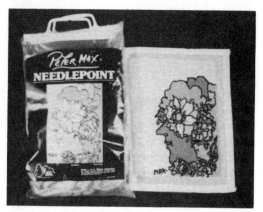

Figure 11–60. Needlepoint Kit, circa 1972. Artistic Creative Needlepoint, Union, NJ. Makes a 14" × 16" finished needlepoint; **$40,** unused; **$30–$50,** made up and finished.

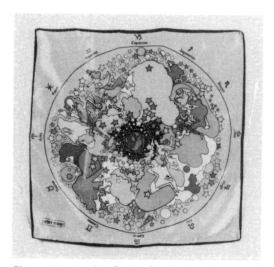

Figure 11–62. Scarf, "Zodiac." circa 1969–70. Blue/orange/purple/green/yellow/pink/dark blue/white; 21" × 21"; **$65–$75.**

Figure 11–63. Scarf, "Cosmic Jump," circa 1969. Silk, Made in Japan. Black/yellow/white/green/pink; $42\frac{1}{4}$" × 14"; **$75.**

(This design also comes with a red background instead of black.)

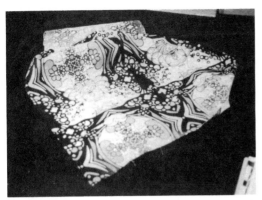

Figure 11–64. Bolt of fabric, circa 1970–71. Dark blue/pink/orange/green/yellow/white/turquoise; **$300–$400.**

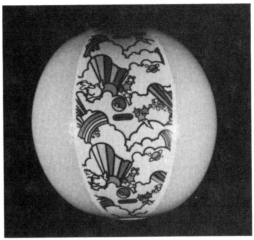

Figure 11–66. Beach ball, inflatable plastic, 1971. Mego Corp. NY, Made in Taiwan; Orange panels alternating with design panels in white/yellow/ blue/orange/green/black/red—also comes with blue panels instead of the orange; 24"; **$35.**

Figure 11–65. Game, Chesset, © 1971. Cardboard board, with cardboard cut-out stand-up playing pieces. Kontrell. Black/white playing area; Playing pieces and box: multi-colors; Board, $23\frac{3}{4}"\times 23\frac{1}{2}"$: Box, $24\frac{1}{4}"\times 12\frac{1}{4}"$; **$150–$200.**

Protest and Politics

Government was a very hot topic in the psychedelic era, and there are many collectible artifacts depicting the various opinions of the time. In addition to the campaign items of the 1968 election, the team of Nixon and Agnew probably inspired more fun-poking items than any other president and vice president so far. Dart boards, clocks and watches, puzzles, garbage cans, posters, and all kinds of silly buttons and figures were made between 1968 and 1973 caricaturing the two candidates.

Today, protests are fairly common, civilized affairs, usually without any violence or arrests. They're generally newsworthy, but protesting isn't what it used to be. The police in Washington, D.C. are as polite to protesters as to any other tourists. Expressing your opinion used to be much more dangerous. You could be beaten, maced, teargassed, set upon by police dogs, arrested, or shot at. At the Chicago Democratic convention, in 1968, police surrounded the protesters completely, then proceeded to beat as many of them as possible. One of the worst cases was a protest rally at Kent State in 1970. Four people were killed when National Guardsmen fired at the crowd.

There isn't much variety in protest items. Buttons which were worn by many of the marchers, and some leaflets do surface. Rarest are the protest posters. Most were quick, cheap printings, done with one or two colors on thin paper. They were not made to last long, and most of them didn't. The majority have simple graphics and, unlike the popular music posters, are very readable.

Collecting Hints

 Although at times expensive, political items are relatively available. But if your interest is in protest items, you may find them difficult to get. I'd recommend trying to obtain a copy of *Prop Art* (See chapter 1). It depicts posters you may not be able to find for sale.

There are no reproductions of these things, yet.

Figure 12–1. Poster, "Turn Off, Tune Out, Drop In," © 1967 (see color section). Astro Posters, Berkeley, CA, #7. John Thompson, artist. Blue/white/red; $18\frac{15}{16}$" × $24\frac{15}{16}$"; **$75–$100.**

Figure 12–3. Poster, "Here and Now for Bobby Seale," 1970. Black Panther Party. Black on orange paper; $17\frac{1}{16}$" × 22"; No recent sale information.

Figure 12–2. Poster, "Avenge (Kent State)," 1970. Black/white; 22" × 17"; No recent sale information.

Figure 12–4. Poster, "Bring the Troops Home Now," 1967 (see color section). Student Mobilization Committee, NY. Nancy Coner, artist. Black/red/orange; 17⅞" × 22⅞"; No recent sale information.

Figure 12–6. Poster, "Join the Conspiracy, Oct. 8–11," 1970. Mark Morris, Designer; for the Conspiracy, Chicago, Illinois. Black/white; 17¹⁵⁄₁₆" × 23¹⁵⁄₁₆"; No recent sale information.

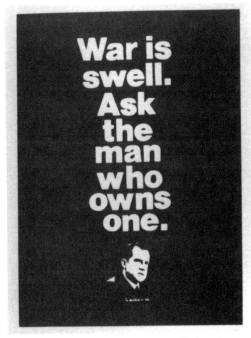

Figure 12–5. Poster, "War is swell. Ask the man who owns one." 1970. Black/white; 16¹³⁄₁₆" × 22¹⁵⁄₁₆"; No recent sale information.

Figure 12–7. Poster, "Augusta—He only made page 5," 1970. Printed on New York University stationery. Blue/white; 16¹⁵⁄₁₆" × 22"; No recent sale information.

Figure 12–8. Poster, "McCarthy is Happening,"
May 25, 1968. Santa Clara County Fairgrounds,
Calif. Elmore, artist. Blue on brown paper; $12\frac{5}{16}$" ×
$29\frac{13}{16}$"; No recent sale information. A good guess
might be **$200–$300.**

Figure 12–9. Poster, "Conference on the Draft,"
May 27, 1967, San Francisco, Cal. Also—Gut,
artist. Red/blue/white; 14" × 20"; **$100.**

Figure 12–10. Poster, "Ronnie is my choice in
'68." Posters Inc., 1967, Holyoke, Mass. Yellow/
green/red/maroon/white/black; $23\frac{1}{8}$" × $35\frac{1}{8}$"; **$65.**

Figure 12−11. Button, "April 15 SMC" (Student Mobilization Committee). White/black/red; 1¾"; **$10−$15.**

Figure 12−12. Button, "Out Now, Nov. 6th," Demonstrate Against the War. NPAC (National Peace Action Coalition). Orange/yellow/blue; 1¾"; **$10−$15.**

Figure 12−13. Button, "Out Now." Student Mobilization Committee to End the War in Vietnam. White/black; 2½"; **$10−$15.**

Figure 12−14. Button, "Bring the Troops Home Now," circa 1967. N.G. Slater Corp., NYC. White/black; 1½"; **$10−$15.**

Figure 12−15. Button, "March on Boston—Keep the Buses Rolling," 1975. N.G. Slater Corp., NYC. White/black; 2¼"; **$10.**

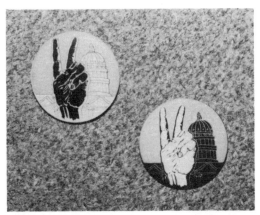

Figure 12−16. Buttons, Peace/Washington, circa 1969. New Mobilization Committee, Washington, DC. Horn Co., Phila., Pa. Black/white/blue; 2½"; **$10−$15** each.

The button with the black hand is a little rarer.

Figure 12–17. Button, Peace. The Button Man, Detroit, Mich. Black/white; 1½"; **$10–$15.**

Figure 12–18. Button, "March on Washington—San Francisco, April 24—Out Now—NPAC," (National Peace Action Colition), 1971. Yellow/blue/red; 1⅝"; **$15–$20.**

Figure 12–19. Button, "War is not healthy for children and other living things," circa 1971. White/black/pink/orange/green; 3½"; **$10.**

Figure 12–20. Button, "Retire J. Edgar Hoover," 1968. Orange/yellow; 1¼"; **$8–$10.**

Figure 12–21. Buttons, "Peace Now," circa 1971. Blue/white; 2¼"; **$5–$10** each.

Figure 12–22. Button, "War is not healthy for children and other living things." Jomoco, 383 Fifth Ave., NYC. White/black/green/orange/pink; 2⅛" square; **$15–$20.**

Figure 12–23. Buttons, Nixon. 1. "Nixon's the one!" 1968. White/black; **$10.** 2. "Nixon's still the one in '72!" 1972. White/black; **$10.**

Figure 12–24. Button, Nixon. "Nixon drinks Ripple—Boycott Gallo Wines." Orange/black; 1½"; **$10.**

Figure 12–25. Button, Spiro Agnew, circa 1970. "Spiro our hero." White/blue/red; 1¾"; **$12.**

Figure 12–26. Button, McGovern, 1972. "Carole King, Barbra Streisand, James Taylor. McGovern—Use the power—18 register and vote." White/brown; 3½"; **$75–$100.**

Figure 12–27. Buttons, McGovern, 1972. 1. Smilie "McGovern." White/black/red; 1⅜"; **$12–$15.** 2. "For Peace McGovern." White/black/blue; 1¼"; **$10.**

Figure 12–28. Button, 1972. "Keep on truckin'... with Muskie." White/blue/red; 3½"; **$20.**

Figure 12–29. Button, Ronald Reagan, 1968. "Had Enough?" Black/white; 1¼"; **$8–$10.**

Figure 12–30. Patch: Agnew, circa 1970. White/blue/red/gold; 3½"; **$5–$10.**

Figure 12–32. Bracelet: POW/MIA, 1970. **$10–$20.**

Figure 12–33. Political pamphlet for Senator Eugene J. McCarthy, 1968. 12 pages. Black/white; **$20.**

Figure 12–31. Pin, Nixon. "No more bull—Peace now!" Black/white; 3"; **$15.**

Figure 12–34. Puzzle, Nixon & Agnew, © 1970. "This is a two-faced jigsaw puzzle" (picture on both sides). The Puzzle Factory, NY, NY. White/blue/red/black; 12¼" × 8¼", box; 21¾" × 14¾", puzzle; **$25–$30.**

Figure 12–35. Dart board: Nixon, circa 1970. Seed Associates, Salem, NH. White/blue/red; 15" × 15"; **$45–$75.**

Figure 12–38. Dartboard: Spiro Agnew, circa 1971. Black/white; $14\frac{1}{8}$"; **$35–$40.**

Figure 12–36. Clock: Spiro Agnew, circa 1970. Dirty Time Company. Orange case, white/blue/red/black face, gold bells and feet; 4" tall; **$125.**

Figure 12–39. Puzzle, Spiro Agnew, 1970. Gameophiles Ltd., Berkeley Heights, NJ. Multicolor; $9\frac{1}{4}$" × $13\frac{1}{8}$", box; 16" × 20", puzzle; **$20–$25.**

Figure 12–37. Clock: Nixon, "Super Dick," circa 1972. Lendan. Made in USA. White/black/blue/red/yellow/pink; 9"; **$85–$125.**

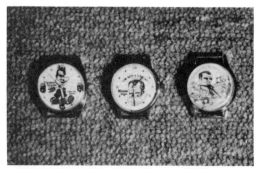

Figure 12–40. Watches: Nixon. 1. Dickey Nixon Official, circa 1970–71. Dirty Time Company. White/blue/red/flesh/black, silver-colored case; **$125.** 2. Nixon says . . . "I'm not a crook" (His eyes move with the seconds), circa 1974. Honest Time Co. White/blue/red/flesh/black, face; gold-colored case; **$150.** 3. Watergate—Oops! Beg pardon! You're pardoned, circa 1974. Honest Time Co. Green/white/flesh/blue/red/black, face; gold-colored case; **$100.**

Figure 12–42. Plastic figure: Nixon, made to hang in car window, circa 1970. Black/flesh/white/red; $3\frac{7}{8}$"; **$30.**

Figure 12–41. Watches; Spiro Agnew, all circa 1970. 1. Spiro Agnew original. Dirty Time Co. White/red/blue/black/flesh; gold-colored case; **$110–$125.** 2. Spiro Who? White/yellow/red/blue/flesh; gold-colored case; **$75.** 3. Official Spiro Agnew Watch. C.E.G.T.C. White/blue/red; gold-colored case; **$75.** 4. Super Star. Bradley Time. White/blue/red/yellow; silver-colored case; **$75.** 5. Spiro. White/black/red/blue; **$75.**

Figure 12–43. Candle, Nixon, circa 1971. Flesh/black/brown; $6\frac{1}{2}$" tall; **$20.**

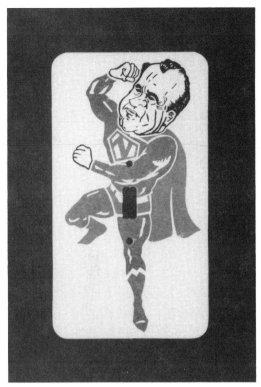

Figure 12–44. Switch-plate cover: Super Dick, circa 1972. White/blue/red/black; 5″ × 8¾″; **$25.**

Figure 12–45. Ronald Reagan watch, circa 1970. Fraxe Co. White/blue/black/red/brown; **$125.**

Figure 12–46. Mug, "Bobby for President," 1968. White/blue/red; 4″ tall; **$15–$25.**

Smilies

Smilies started to appear around 1968–69, and really blossomed from 1971 to 1974. The happy face was everywhere. Where did it come from and who designed it? Nobody seems to know exactly. There was no copyright on it, so it was used freely by any manufacturer. I have a theory that it was probably originally a sun symbol, since most smilies are yellow. But what a perfect graphic design. Smilies have no particular language, race, or sex. They make no comment on politics. They can't offend anybody. It's just a smile which anyone can understand. When placed on merchandise, it sold. After all, everybody likes to see a smiling face, right? So the manufacturers made lots and lots of smilie things. But then they stopped around 1975. I guess it became a cliché. People started to say "have a nice day" with too much sarcasm. Oh well—Have a nice day!

Collecting Hints

 There are some new smilie things available, but they are not exactly reproductions. New merchandise includes T-shirts, a really nice wrist watch with a smilie face, and a few items in jewelry. (And a gross T-shirt with a hole in his head.) Some of the new things include the phrase "Don't Worry—Be Happy," which wasn't used in the '70s.

*Figure 13-1. Bags, blue denim. 1. Yellow printed design; 12" long; **$10-$15**. 2. Sewn-on yellow and blue patch; 7½" long; **$6-$10**.*

*Figure 13-2. Bank, plastic. Yellow/black; 5½" tall; **$10-$15**.*

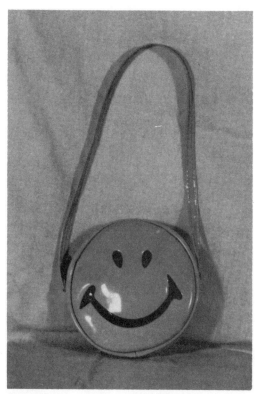

*Figure 13-3. Handbag, vinyl. Yellow/black; 7" (not including the handle); **$30-$45**.*

*Figure 13-4. Luggage, vinyl. Yellow/black; 11⅝" × 11"; **$30-$50**.*

Figure 13−5. Tote bag, plastic. Yellow/black; 11"
(not including the handle); **$15.**

Figure 13−6. Tote bag, plastic. Clear/black/yellow;
14½" (not including the handles); **$15.**

Figure 13−7. Bank, pottery. Yellow/black; 6" tall;
$15−$20.

Figure 13−8. Ice bucket, metal. Yellow/cream/
black; 10½" (not including the handle); **$25−$30.**

Figure 13-9. Banks, plastic. 1. Yellow/black/red; 7"; **$10.** 2. Yellow/white/black/red; 11"; **$15-$20.**

Figure 13-11. Tray, metal. White/yellow/black; $12\frac{1}{2}$" × $17\frac{1}{4}$"; **$15-$20.**

Figure 13-10. Cocktail Set. "Hazelware," glass with chrome shaker lid. Clear glass with yellow, red, green, or blue smilies; 9" shaker, $3\frac{1}{2}$" glasses; **$30-$40.**

Figure 13-12. Tray, metal. "Happiness is Paragon Park." Nanco, Boston, Mass. Black/white; $12\frac{1}{4}$"; **$10.**

Figure 13-13. Plastic mat. Yellow/black; 12"; **$10-$15.**

Figure 13–14. Cookie Jar. McCoy Pottery Co. Yellow/black; 11"; **$25–$30.**

Figure 13–15. Salt and Pepper Shakers, pottery. Treasure Craft, USA. Green/black, 2½"; **$20.**

Figure 13–17. Mug. McCoy Pottery Co. Yellow/black; 3¾"; **$6–$10.**

Figure 13–18. Dish Towel, cotton cloth, hung on a dowel. White/pink/blue/yellow/black; 25¾" × 17"; **$15.**

Figure 13–16. Glasses. Clear glass with yellow, green, red, or blue smilies; 1. 6¾". 2. 5½ ". 3.5". **$6–$12** each.

*Figure 13–19. Plate and mug, hard plastic. Yellow/ black; Plate, 10"; mug, 4". Plate, **$10–$15;** mug, **$5–$10.***

*Figure 13–22. Pillow, cotton. Blue, green, red, or yellow/black design; 12" × 12"; **$10** each.*

*Figure 13–20. Flower pot. McCoy Pottery Co. Yellow/black; 4½"; **$10–$15.***

*Figure 13–23. Waste can, metal. Cheinco, Made in USA. White/yellow/black; 13" tall; **$20.***

*Figure 13–21. Candle mold, aluminum. 6" (makes a 5" candle); **$20.***

Figure 13–24. Waste can, metal. J.V. Reed & Co., Louisville, Ky. Pink/yellow/black; 9½"; **$20–$25.**

Figure 13–25. Note Paper. Yellow/black; 10½" × 10½", box; **$8–$15.**

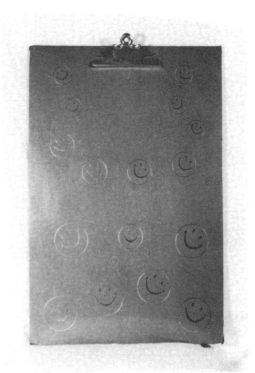

Figure 13–27. Clip-board, Vinyl on masonite. Green/metallic gold; 16" × 24"; **$10.**

Figure 13–28. Pencil Sharpener, plastic and metal. Berol, Made in USA. Yellow/black; 5" tall; **$25–$30.**

Figure 13–26. Note Paper. Pratt & Austin Co., Holyoke, Mass. Pink/turquoise/orange/yellow/black/white; 7¾" × 8⅛", box; **$8–$15.**

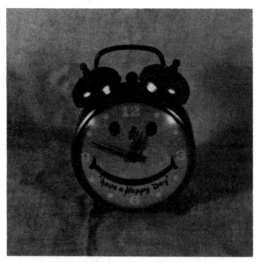

Figure 13–29. Alarm clock. Robert Shaw Controls Co., Lux Time Div. Lebanon, Tenn. Metal case. Yellow/red/white/black/brass bells; $5\frac{3}{4}$" tall; **$30–$50.**

Figure 13–31. Rug, plush. Yellow/black; 26"; **$25–$40.**

Figure 13–30. Wall clock, plastic case. Robert Shaw Controls Co., Lux Time Div. Lebanon, Tenn. USA. Yellow/white/black; 7"; **$25–$45.**

Figure 13–32. Light. Black light (actually purple/white enameled design on black base. Westinghouse. $7\frac{1}{2}$" tall; **$10–$15.**

Figure 13–33. Bumper Sticker. Black/yellow; $3\frac{3}{4}$" × $14\frac{5}{8}$"; **$10,** unused.

Figure 13-34. Poster, 1971. Black/yellow; 22" × 34"; **$25-$35.**

Figure 13-36. Night light. Green/black (probably came in other colors also); 4¾"; **$20-$30.**

Figure 13-37. Doll, stuffed, plush cloth with satin ribbon. Commonwealth Toy Co. Inc., Brooklyn, N.Y. Yellow/black, pink/blue ribbon; 15" tall; **$15-$20.**

Figure 13-35. Doll, stuffed cotton cloth with printed design. Orange/black; 16" tall; **$15-$20.**

Figure 13–38. Toy toaster, plastic. Empire Plastic Corp., N.C. Yellow/black; 4" tall; **$10–$20.**

Figure 13–40. Jewelry. Top row: 1. Pin, yellow enamel on gold-colored metal. **$5–$10.** 2. Pin, unusual rhinestone. **$20–$25.** 3. Pendant, yellow enamel on metal. **$5–$10.** Bottom row: 1. Necklace, yellow enamel on gold-colored metal. **$5–$10.** 2. Earrings, yellow enamel on metal. **$10.** 3. Pendant, silver metal with plastic moving googlie eyes. **$15.**

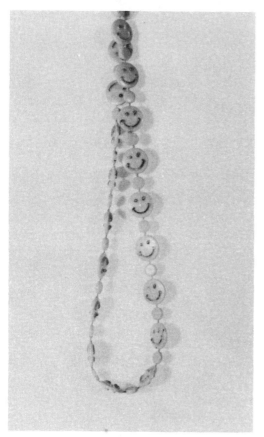

Figure 13–39. Necklace, molded plastic. Yellow, pink, orange, or blue; 20" or 30"; **$15–$20.**

Figure 13–41. Pins and Buttons. **$5–$15** each.

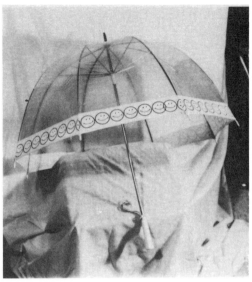

Figure 13-43. Umbrella, plastic. Clear/white/yel-low; **$30-$50.**

Figure 13-42. Dress, top and mini skirt, polyester, circa 1974. Brown with smilies in orange/pink/white; **$25-$50.**

Toys And Other Stuff . . .

14

Although "personality" toys, featuring the Beatles, Monkees, and various other pop idols have been made for decades, it wasn't until the early 1970s that the major toy manufacturers decided to capitalize on pop culture in general. Then there was an avalanche of hippie figures and dolls, (even Ken grew his hair longer!), "Mod" fashion dolls, and various toys and games. There was even a game called "LSD" (it's a puzzle-game), and the puzzle manufacturers tried to drive people crazy with op-art patterns and psychedelic designs. You could create your own psychedelic art with a Spirograph, Pendulart, or a Spin-Art.

Other toys can be found listed in Chapter 11, Peter Max; Chapter 6, Movies and Theater (Yellow Submarine); Chapter 12, Protest and Politics; Chapter 13, Smilies; Chapter 7, Television (Monkees, Laugh-In).

The "other stuff" in this chapter is

comprised of all the neat items that don't seem to fit in any other place in the book. In a way, *all* collectibles are toys, since a toy is an unnecessary item used for entertainment. When you get down to it people collect things—rare glassware, fine art, or baseball cards—because collecting is interesting—it's fun. So, have fun with your toys, whatever they are!

Collecting Hints

 There are books specifically on the subject of dolls and collecting them. You may want to refer to the chapter in this book about Clothing to familiarize yourself with the styles you may find on dolls. It's pretty easy to spot psychedelic and mod toys. Most of these things were made only for a short time, and have not been reproduced. The only toy that survived the psychedelic era is the spirograph, which is still being made.

Figure 14–2. Checker board, masonite with wood frame. Quite Contrary Inc. NY. Black/white; 18¾" × 31"; $45–$55.

Figure 14–1. Chess Set, colored cast Lucite. Green/ blue; 18" × 18", board; 1¾" to 3½" tall, pieces. $150.

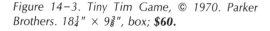

Figure 14–3. Tiny Tim Game, © 1970. Parker Brothers. 18¼" × 9⅜", box; $60.

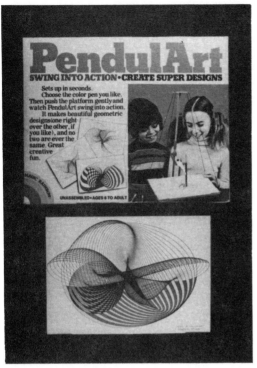

Figure 14–4. Drawing toy, PendulArt, circa 1970. Magran Industries, Vernon, Calif. $10.
This creates psychedelic designs.

Figure 14–5. Music Box, plastic. Made in Japan. Green/blue/clear plastic/red; 3" square; $40.
Bottom plastic disk rotates while playing "Goin' out of my head."

Figure 14–6. Peeing hippie, plastic, circa 1970. Made in Hong Kong. Brown/blue/red/pink; 6" tall; $20–$30.

Figure 14–7. "Dawk" (Cousin It influenced figure), plastic and yarn. Yellow/brown/blue/black; 10" tall; $35.

Figure 14-8. Tiny Tim trolls, circa 1969. 1. Black pants, black and white shirt, brown hair. 2. Black suit, orange hair. 3½" tall; **$100-$125** each.

Figure 14-10. Dolls and Case, "Rock Flowers," 1970. Mattel, Hawthorne, Calif. 6½" tall, dolls; 9⅝" × 6½", case; **$45** a set.

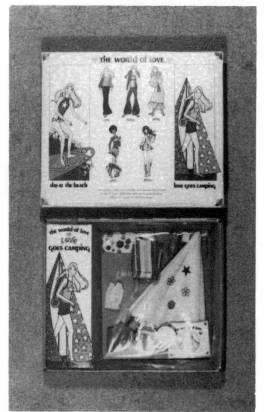

Figure 14-9. Playsets, "World of Love," 1972. Hasbro Industries. Dolls: "Love," "Peace," "Flower," "Soul," and "Music." Playsets: "Love's Own Room," "Love's Day at the Beach," "Love Goes Camping." **$20** each, dolls; **$15** each, playsets.

Figure 14-11. Doll, Flip Wilson/Geraldine, cloth, 1970. Shindana Toys. 15" tall; **$35.**

Figure 14–12. Doll, "Mimi" (in original clothes) with fasion sets, 1973. Remco Industries Inc., Harrison, NJ. 19" tall, doll; **$45, $20** each fashion set.

Figure 14–13. Dolls, Chrissy and Velvet, with card showing their clothes and boxes for other dolls, 1972. Ideal Toy Corp., Hollis, NY. 18" tall, Chrissy; 16" tall, Velvet. **$40** each.

Figure 14–14. Kit, Mod Rod Miniature Car Kit, 1970. Lindberg Products Inc. $3\frac{1}{2}$" × $4\frac{1}{4}$", box; **$15.**

Figure 14–15. Puzzles "Thingies," 1968. Springbok Editions, Inc. Sandy Miller, artist. 7", puzzles; $4\frac{1}{4}$", boxes. **$10** each.

Figure 14–16. Set of decals. Various colors; $8\frac{1}{8}$" × $10\frac{3}{16}$" sheet; **$15** a set.

Figure 14–17. Record Case for 33's, cardboard, covered in psychedelic patterned paper, circa 1968. Pink/white/gray; 12¾" × 13" × 4¾"; **$10–$15.**

Figure 14–19. Radio, 1971. Realistic. Blue/yellow/red/white; 3⅞"; **$45–$50.**

Figure 14–20. Radios, plastic, circa 1971. Panasonic. Red, yellow, or white; 4", round ones; 5¼" × 3⅞", cubes; 6", doughnuts. **$45–$50.**

Figure 14–18. Telephone, promotional plastic display model (not functional). Blue/white/red/gold; 35" tall; **$350.**

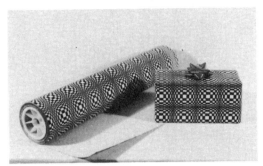

Figure 14–21. Op Art Wrapping Paper, circa 1970–71. Black/white; 24" wide, on a large roll; **$100–$150,** roll.

Figure 14–22. Postcards—Small Faces first American Tour. Warner Brothers Records, Calif. Red/black/blue, bus; black/white, British flag. **$20** each.

Figure 14–24. Stationery, circa 1972. Yellow paper; multicolor envelopes. $9\frac{1}{4}$" × $8\frac{1}{4}$", paper; **$8–$10.**

Figure 14–25. New Years Centerpiece, paper, circa 1970–72. Hallmark Cards, Inc. Purple/red/blue/white; 13" tall; **$15–$20.**

Figure 14–23. Writing paper, "Mod", circa 1968–69. Lingco, Tenn. Flourescent pink/yellow/orange/green; $7\frac{3}{4}$" × $10\frac{3}{4}$"; **$10–$15,** unused.

Figure 14–26. Matchbook, circa 1968. Superior Match Co. Chicago, USA. Pink/black; 4" × 1½"; **$10.**

Figure 14–27. Card, (for the clothing shop Granny Takes a Trip, London and New York). 3¾" × 6"; **$20–$25.**

Figure 14–28. Paper bag and card, circa 1971. Baltimore Head shops, "The Bum Steer Ltd." and "Ward's Folly." Orange/black, bag; white/red/black, card. **$10,** bag; **$5–$10,** card.

Figure 14–29. Pen, Twiggy, (on original card), circa 1968. Scripto. 7½" tall, card; **$15.**

Figure 14–30. Pens (on original card), circa 1967. The Swingers. **$30.**

Figure 14–32. Bottle, Avon after shave. Red/silver; 5¾" long; **$10.**

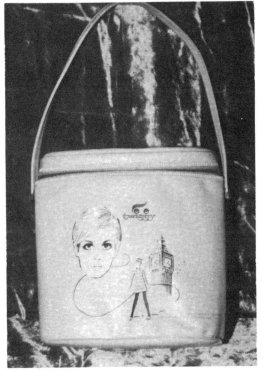

Figure 14–31. Lunch bag and thermos, Twiggy, vinyl, circa 1967. Minnow Co. Ltd., Aladdin Industries Inc., Nashville, Tenn. Lavender/yellow/blue/black/pink; 8" tall (not including the handle); **$40–$60.**

Figure 14–33. Figure, pottery, circa 1971. 404 Berries, 1971, Made in Hong Kong. Green/orange/blue/pink/white/black; 5¼" tall; **$15.**

Figure 14–34. Bank, pottery, circa 1970. Women's Rights. Blue/brown/yellow/pink/red; $6\frac{5}{16}$" tall; **$20.**

Figure 14–35. Note cards, 1971. Alan Hartwell, designer for Random Press, Inc., NY, NY. 1. Ecology, white/green. 2. Life, white/blue/red. 3. Feet, white/blue. 4. Love, red/white. $5\frac{3}{8}$" × $4\frac{1}{4}$" **$5–$10.**

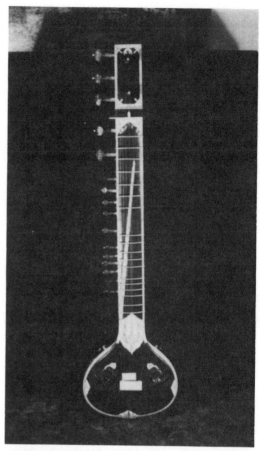

Figure 14–36. Indian Sitar, rosewood, ivory and gourd, circa 1968. 49" tall; **$300.**

Sitars were imported in large numbers between 1967 and 1970. Their popularity was due largely to Ravi Shankar and to the Beatles, who experimented with the sitar. The instrument is extremely difficult to play, which may explain its decline in vogue after 1970.

References

Grushkin, Paul D. *The Art of Rock*. New York: Abbeville Press, 1987.

King, Eric. *A Collector's Guide to the Numbered Dance Posters*. Created for Bill Graham and The Family Dog, 1966–1973. Berkeley: Svaha Press, 1980.

Harris, Jennifer; Hyde, Sarah; and Smith, Greg. *1966 and All That—Design and the Consumer in Britain 1960–1969*. London: Trefoil Books, 1986.

Katz, Sylvia. *Plastics, Common Objects, Classic Designs*. New York: Harry N. Abrams, 1984.

DiNoto, Andrea. *Art Plastic, Designed for Living*. New York: Abbeville Press, 1984.

Fox, Alison. *Rock & Pop—Phillips Collector's Guides*. London: Dunestyle Publishing & Boxtree, 1988.

Note: Many good references are out-of-print, and also collectible. See Chapter 1.

Museums

The Smithsonian
Washington, DC

The Oakland Museum
Oakland, CA

The Museum of Modern Art
New York, NY

The Brooklyn Museum
Brooklyn, NY

The Connecticut Museum of American
Political Life
(the University of Hartford)
Hartford, CT

Shops

Many of the shops listed here will not have all the items discussed in this book. Their stock will vary. And I'm sure there are many other shops that I've not listed. Antique and collectible shows can be a source, as well as Beatles conventions, toy shows, and paper and ephemera shows. There are many dealers who exhibit only at shows and have no shops. And a few who do only mail-order.

Flamingo
495 Main Street
Northpoint, NY 11768

Flashback
102A West Main Street
Carrboro, NC

The Garment District (clothing)
Broad Street
Cambridge, MA

It's Only Rock 'n' Roll
49 West 8th Street
New York, NY 10011

Just Kids
5 Green Street
Huntington Station, NY

Neat Stuff Enterprises
341 South 13th Street
Philadelphia, PA 19107

Psychedelic Solution
33 West 8th Street
New York, NY 10011

Wex Rex
65 Main Street
Hudson, MA 01749

Another source would be the Sotheby's and Christies' Auctions in New York City, and London. The Rock 'n' Roll auctions and Sotheby's "Collector's Carrousel" auctions sometimes have some really great stuff.

Index